ICNC **MONOGRAPH** SERIES

SERIES EDITOR: Maciej Bartkowski
CONTACT: mbartkowski@nonviolent-conflict.org
VOLUME EDITORS: Hardy Merriman, Amber French, Cassandra Balfour
DESIGNED BY: David Reinbold
CONTACT: icnc@nonviolent-conflict.org

Other volumes in this series:
The Power of Staying Put: Nonviolent Resistance against Armed Groups in Colombia, Juan Masullo (2015)

Published by ICNC Press
International Center on Nonviolent Conflict
P.O. Box 27606
Washington, D.C. 20038 USA

© 2015 International Center on Nonviolent Conflict, Tenzin Dorjee
All rights reserved. ISBN: 978-1-943271-01-6

Cover photos: (l) John Ackerly, 1987, (r) Invisible Tibet Blog

John Ackerly's photo of the first major demonstration in Lhasa in 1987 became an emblem for the Tibet movement. The monk Jampa Tenzin, who is being lifted by fellow protesters, had just rushed into a burning police station to rescue Tibetan detainees. With his arms charred by the flames, he falls in and out of consciousness even as he leads the crowd in chanting pro-independence slogans. The photographer John Ackerly became a Tibet advocate and eventually President of the International Campaign for Tibet (1999 to 2009). To read more about John Ackerly's experience in Tibet, see his book co-authored by Blake Kerr, *Sky Burial: An Eyewitness Account of China's Brutal Crackdown in Tibet*.

Invisible Tibet Blog's photo was taken during the 2008 Tibetan uprising when Tibetans across the three historical provinces of Tibet rose up to protest Chinese rule. The protests began on March 10, 2008, a few months ahead of the Beijing Olympic Games, and quickly became the largest, most sustained nonviolent movement Tibet has witnessed.

The designations used and material presented in this publication do not indicate the expression of any opinion whatsoever on the part of ICNC. The author holds responsibility for the selection and presentation of facts contained in this work, as well as for any and all opinions expressed therein, which are not necessarily those of ICNC and do not commit the organization in any way.

The Tibetan Nonviolent Struggle:

A STRATEGIC AND HISTORICAL ANALYSIS

Summary

Contrary to a perception — fueled by Chinese propaganda during the 2008 Tibetan uprising — that the Tibetan struggle is heading toward extremism, this study shows that the movement has since the 1950s moved toward a tighter embrace of nonviolent resistance. This monograph investigates three major Tibetan uprising periods and analyzes their central themes, purposes, challenges, strategies, tactics and impacts. The first uprising (1956-59) was predominantly violent; the second (1987-89) was largely nonviolent but confined to the Tibetan capital Lhasa; the third (2008) was predominantly nonviolent and spread to all three historical provinces of Tibet. An era of cultural renaissance preceded both the second and third uprisings, laying the groundwork that emboldened and prepared the people to seek political freedom through collective action.

Until recently, Tibetans conceptualized their commitment to nonviolent resistance in purely moral terms, but today this principled outlook is being replaced by a more strategic approach that views nonviolent struggle as a weapon to be wielded with a degree of planning, discipline and organizing rather than merely as a moral ideal.

The Tibetan leadership has pursued a strategy that relies heavily on building international diplomatic pressure on China, aimed at achieving change for Tibet through some form of conversion of opponents' views and values rather than nonviolent coercion. But to increase their chances of success Tibetans must recalibrate their strategy to harness not only international influence, but also domestic social, economic and political forces. By mobilizing these internal strengths, Tibetans can multiply the pressure on China, which is the only way to move a regime that has proven unlikely to be persuaded.

Today, Tibetans are engaging in a growing noncooperation movement. In the aftermath of the 2008 uprising, China tried to eradicate all signs of dissent in the streets by turning Tibet into a police state. But the millions of dollars China spent on the militarization and securitization of the Tibetan plateau failed to make the revolution disappear; it only made it move indoors, embedding the resistance firmly in the daily lives of the residents. Tibetans are channeling their spirit of resistance into social, cultural and economic activities that are noncooperative (refusing to support Chinese institutions and businesses) and self-constructive (promoting Tibetan language and other self-reliance and cultural capital-building activities which constitute what the author calls 'transformative resistance'). This is all happening in an immensely repressive political environment, which shows that there is a way to mobilize people power against even one of the most ruthless regimes in the world.

Photo credit: Jimmy Tran/Shutterstock

Table of Contents

Abstract	5
Introduction	9
Chapter 1: Literature Review	11
Strategic Nonviolent Theory as a Framework	13
Contents of this Monograph	15
Key Arguments	16
Chapter 2: Historical Background	19
Ancient Tibet	19
Chinese Invasion	23
Buddhism, Nonviolence and Gandhi	25
Chapter 3: The First Tibetan Uprising (1956-59)	27
Armed Rebellion in Eastern Tibet in 1956	27
1959 Lhasa Uprising	24
The CIA's Tibet Connection	35
Renunciation of Violence	36
Chapter 4: Internationalization in Exile — Liberalization in Tibet (1980s)	37
In Exile: A New Strategy to 'Internationalize' the Tibet Issue	37
In Tibet: A Period of Liberalization (1980-87)	38
Chapter 5: The Second Tibetan Uprising (1987-89)	43
Protests and Riots in Lhasa – 1987	43
Analyzing the Strategy and Tactics of the Uprising	45
Street Demonstration	46
Poster Campaigns	48
Distribution of Literature	49
Graffiti	49
Kora – Circumambulation	50
Protest Singing	50
Noncooperation	51
Chapter 6: The Rise and Fall of Global Grassroots Mobilization (1989-2002)	53
Legislative Support in the West	53
Global Grassroots Mobilization and the Rise of Pro-Tibet NGOs	54
Start of Dialogue, End of Mobilization	57
Chapter 7: The Third Uprising (2008)	61
Cultural Preparation for Political Mobilization	61
2008: Nationwide Protests, Lhasa Riots	66
Nonviolent Discipline, Strategy and Unity	66
The Lhakar Movement: Cultural Resistance	67
Parallel Institution-Building	69
Noncooperation	69
Chapter 8: A Comparison of the Three Uprisings	71
Chapter 9: Strategic Challenges and Transformative Resistance	77
Nonviolent Credo and Existing Strategic Challenges	77
Transformative Resistance	79
Chapter 10: Recommendations for Domestic and External Actors	81
What Foreign Actors Can Do	83
What the Tibetan Leadership Can Do	86
Cited Literature	90
List of Figures	94

Introduction

The Tibetan freedom movement occupies an iconic place in the popular imagination as the ultimate David-versus-Goliath struggle. Here is Tibet: an ancient nation of 6 million people trying to regain their ancestral homeland on the "Roof of the World."[1] There is China: a modern empire with the world's largest population, the second largest economy, and the largest standing army.

In a world wrecked by violent conflict, the Tibetan self-determination struggle has long been applauded for its commitment to nonviolent discipline. Yet following the 2008 riots in the Tibetan capital Lhasa, observers have remarked that the Tibetan struggle is turning violent towards occupiers, and that through the rise of self-immolations, Tibetans are also inflicting violence against themselves.[2] The national uprising of 2008 was portrayed in the mainstream media as a sign of militant Tibetan youth renouncing the nonviolent principles of the Dalai Lama — a new generation discarding the pacifist ideals of an older generation. The media churned out sensational headlines: "Young Tibetans question path of nonviolence,"[3] "Exiles question Dalai Lama's nonviolence,"[4] and "Violence in Tibet as monks clash with the police."[5] The riots, captured on Chinese surveillance cameras, were broadcast repeatedly on domestic and international television channels, launching a new narrative that Tibetans were in fact bound to resort to violence and that their supposedly nonviolent image was a cover for terrorist actions.

There are many lingering questions such as, is the Tibetan struggle truly growing radicalized and violent? Which strategies and tactics is it really using? When and how did

---

[1] The elevation of the Tibetan Plateau averages between 15,000 and 16,000 feet (4,570 to 4,880 meters), making it the highest country in the world, hence its nickname "Roof of the World."
[2] Although self-immolations are a critically important subject of discussion, the topic remains outside the scope of this monograph.
[3] Jason Motlagh, "Young Tibetans question path of nonviolence," *The Christian Science Monitor*, 1 April 2008, http://www.csmonitor.com/World/Asia-Pacific/2008/0401/p01s01-woap.html.
[4] Geeta Pandey, "Exiles question Dalai Lama's nonviolence," *BBC News*, 18 March 2008, http://news.bbc.co.uk/2/hi/south_asia/7302661.stm.
[5] Jim Yardley, "Violence in Tibet as monks clash with the police," *The New York Times*, 15 March 2008, http://www.nytimes.com/2008/03/15/world/asia/15tibet.html.

the Tibetan nonviolent resistance come into existence? How has the Tibetan struggle evolved? What roles did nonviolent resistance play in the three major Tibetan uprisings in the late 20th and early 21st centuries? What were the central themes, purposes, challenges, strategies, tactics, tools and impacts in each of the uprisings? What key lessons should Tibetan activists draw from past and recent resistance to better inform their planning and to develop strategies for current and future actions? To answer these questions, one must examine the evolution of the Tibetan resistance over a period of six decades.

In this monograph, I will explore these questions by discussing the birth and evolution of the Tibetan nonviolent resistance movement from the 1950s to present through the lens of strategic nonviolent conflict. The monograph will focus on strategies and tactics employed by the movement over the course of three uprisings: the first uprising from 1956-59, the second from 1987-89 (though the series of protests continued until 1993), and the third in 2008. For the sake of clarity, I will use the term "principled nonviolence" to describe the Dalai Lama's moral and ethical commitment to nonviolent dialogue and mutual compromise; the term "nonviolent resistance" to describe the improvised and spontaneous nonviolent activities during the uprisings; and the term "strategic nonviolent struggle" to describe the strategic and organized application of nonviolent civil resistance.

The research methodology combines secondary data analysis (including archival data) with qualitative methods of author participation and observation of the Tibetan nonviolent struggle, as well as interviews with a number of key Tibetan analysts and actors (many of whom are in exile), over the course of several years. Research was conducted in Tibetan and English.

Chapter 1
Literature Review

There is an extremely small body of literature on the role of nonviolent resistance in the Tibetan struggle. While some have studied the subject in anthropological terms, few have examined it in sociopolitical terms. The majority of the literature on the Tibet issue tends to focus on China's policies in Tibet and the high-level diplomatic tug of war between Beijing, the Chinese capital, and Dharamsala, the seat of the Tibetan government in exile. The various grassroots-level initiatives and nonviolent campaigns by the Tibetan public have hardly received any academic attention.

One of the few published works that analyzes the nonviolent tactics used in the Tibet movement is a short report published by Nonviolence International in 2002. Titled *Truth is Our Only Weapon*, it contains a comprehensive list of nonviolent tactics used by Tibetans in their struggle. There are a handful of other works that discuss the civil resistance aspect of the Tibet movement – Ronald Schwartz's *Circle of Protest: Political Ritual in the Tibetan Uprising* (1995) is one example. However, these publications analyze Tibetan resistance tactics predominantly from an anthropological perspective rather than through the prism of nonviolent conflict.

There are comparatively more works of scholarship on the history of Tibetan armed resistance, including *The Orphans of the Cold War* (1999) by Kenneth Knaus, *Arrested Histories* (2010) by Carole McGranahan, *Buddha's Warriors* (2004) by Mikel Dunham, *The Secret CIA War in Tibet* (2002) by Kenneth Conboy and James Morrison, *Into Tibet* (2002) by Thomas Laird. A Google search today (in August 2015) on "Tibetan armed resistance" yields 495,000 results, while a search on "Tibetan nonviolent resistance" yields not even a third of this (150,000 results). The combination "Tibet + violence" turns up a whopping 996,000 search results while "Tibet + nonviolence" produces 264,000 results.

One reason for this imbalance between writing on armed and unarmed resistance may be the high threshold Tibetans traditionally use to define resistance. In a place where acts such as self-immolations have become a routine part of resistance, less dramatic tactics of resistance such as self-reliance, mutual aid or noncooperation and

civil disobedience do not make a splash. There is an unspoken belief among Tibetans that resistance must involve an act of commission rather than one of omission.[6] Many acts of omission – such as noncooperation with higher authorities, the boycott of Chinese-owned businesses, refusal to attend state schools and rejection of social institutions – are seldom celebrated as resistance, and they often go unnoticed and undocumented. In the Tibetan mindset, only acts of commission that are visible and action-oriented[7] – protest demonstrations, marches and vigils, the chanting of slogans, waving the national flag – are worthy of being counted and documented as acts of resistance. This rather narrow conceptualization of nonviolent resistance has been a major obstacle to the comprehensive documentation of civil resistance in Tibet.

People have a natural tendency to romanticize battles, glorify victories, dramatize defeats, memorialize heroes and demonize enemies. Tibetans are no exception. In the stories of resistance that are passed down to Tibetan children, warriors like Gonpo Tashi and Yurupon and the valiant battles they fought in the 1950s against the Chinese are remembered with reverence and fascination. Nonviolent resistance, on the other hand, does not arouse the same kind of awe, nor does it easily lend itself to visualization or dramatization. Some of the most effective nonviolent campaigns in past independence struggles were built on acts of omission – US colonies' non-exportation and non-importation of British-made products, and the Indian boycott of British textiles come to mind – and are therefore difficult to capture on film or in photos, which are some of the most effective mediums for invoking emotion.

"Glorified violence in the annals of nations, the gendered nature of violence wielded by men, state independence that is seen as having been founded largely on violence, and human attention and media focus all dim the light on the quiet, nonviolent resistance of millions," writes Maciej Bartkowski in *Recovering Nonviolent History*.[8] "This

---

[6] "Acts of omission [occur when] people refuse to perform acts expected by norms, custom, law or decree; [...] acts of commission [occur when] people perform acts that they do not usually perform, are not expected by norms or customs to perform, or are forbidden by law, regulation or decree to perform." Kurt Schock, *Unarmed Insurrections* (Minneapolis: University of Minnesota Press, 2005).

[7] When asked about their role in the resistance, Tibetans would often reply to the author, with a hint of embarrassment, that they were not able to take part in it. But upon closer questioning, the people who claim that they were inactive actually participated in numerous acts of economic noncooperation, social boycott and other acts of omission. This illustrates the Tibetan tendency to equate acts of omission with inaction, simply because both are out of public sight. In reality, acts of omission couldn't be more different from inaction.

[8] Maciej J. Bartkowski, "Recovering Nonviolent History," in *Recovering Nonviolent History: Civil Resistance in Liberation Struggles*, ed. Maciej J. Bartkowski (Boulder: Lynne Rienner Publishers, 2013), 1.

type of struggle neither captures the headlines nor sinks into people's memories unless it provokes the regime's response and, more often than not, a violent one." For many foreign scholars of Tibetan history and politics, the brief chapter of armed resistance in the Tibetan struggle is a captivating subject because of the Central Intelligence Agency's (CIA) involvement in it. The strangeness of the partnership between Tibetan guerrillas and the CIA, which continues to shock students of history, captures the intrigue of historians of Tibet. This results in a narrative of Tibetan history that, at a minimum, deemphasizes nonviolent resistance or, at worst, ignores it all together.

Strategic Nonviolent Theory as a Framework

Nonviolent movements for freedom and democracy over the last decade, particularly during the Arab Spring, brought the subject of civil resistance some long overdue attention from global media, scholars and practitioners. Groups such as the International Center on Nonviolent Conflict (ICNC) and the Albert Einstein Institution (AEI) have supported a growing body of research and literature on strategic nonviolent conflict. This trend received a major boost from the 2011 publication of a groundbreaking study, *Why Civil Resistance Works: The Strategic Logic of Nonviolent Conflict*, by Erica Chenoweth and Maria J. Stephan. The study, which involved rigorous research and quantitative analysis of 323 movements over the course of a century, concluded that nonviolent movements were more than twice as likely to succeed as armed movements.[9] Many practitioners of nonviolent resistance, including Tibetans, greeted this new study with excitement. It gave them a feeling that their chosen method of resistance was not only morally right but also superior in practice.

In the Tibetan struggle, the discourse on nonviolent action has traditionally been framed in a moral dimension. The Tibetan worldview is steeped in Buddhist morality, which meant that most of the discussions around nonviolence revolved around the moral acceptability of the method rather than its practical effectiveness. The emphasis on principled nonviolence in the Tibetan struggle consistently overshadowed the importance of maximizing the impact of nonviolent action.

---

[9] Some of the books that have been translated into Tibetan are Gene Sharp's *From Dictatorship to Democracy, How Nonviolent Struggle Works*, and *The Power and Practice of Nonviolent Political Struggle*, as well as Steve Crawshaw and John Jackson's *Small Acts of Resistance*. A few Tibetan translations of works related to nonviolent conflict can be downloaded free-of-charge via the Albert Einstein Institution website: http://www.aeinstein.org/tibetan/.

[9-1] Chenoweth, Erica and Maria J. Stephan, Why Civil Resistance Works: The Strategic Logic of Nonviolent Conflict (New York: Columbia University Press, 2011).

Figure 1. Methods of Nonviolent Action

Protest and Persuasion	Noncooperation	Nonviolent Intervention
Symbolic acts of the expression of grievances toward a status quo or in support of desired change.	Social: Acts of limiting or refusal of engagement in typical performance of duties, obedience to and following of established sociocultural conventions and practices. Political: Acts of suspending or refusing to carry on usual forms of political and civic participation. Economic: Acts of suspending or refusing to carry on economic relationships as expected.	Disruptive: Acts designed to directly interject into a normalcy of a given state of affairs by disrupting or preventing established patterns of behavior, institutions, policies and relationships. Creative: Acts designed to interject into a normalcy of a given state of affairs by embarking on resource- or relationship-creating activities that generate new patterns of behavior, institutions, policies or practices.

Source: Gene Sharp's *The Politics of Nonviolent Action* and Maciej Bartkowski's *Recovering Nonviolent History*.

In the last few years, books by Gene Sharp – who divides the methods of nonviolent action into three broad categories (see Figure 1) – and other authors on nonviolent theory have been translated into Tibetan and disseminated in the Tibetan community worldwide.[10] NGOs such as ICNC, Tibet Action Institute and the International Tibet Network translated films (such as *A Force More Powerful* and *Bringing Down a Dictator*) into Tibetan, disseminated the documentaries widely and screened them at community gatherings. Activists and grassroots leaders started receiving and offering workshops and trainings in the theory and practice of strategic nonviolent resistance. These initiatives have created a new interest in strategic nonviolent action in the Tibet movement. The campaigns that Tibetans are waging today demonstrate a deeper understanding of strategic nonviolent conflict, and Tibetan activists today are more willing to view

---

[10] Conversion refers to the process whereby the oppressor willingly agrees to the demands of the oppressed. Accommodation refers to the process whereby the opponent does a cost-benefit analysis and concludes that a compromise settlement is preferable to facing continued resistance. Coercion occurs "when the opponent is forced against its will, to meet the demands of the nonviolent movement." Lastly, disintegration happens when the "opponent is not just coerced, but in addition its system of rule disintegrates and falls apart as a result of sustained, widespread, civilian-based noncooperation and nonviolent disruption." Gene Sharp, *The Politics of Nonviolent Conflict*.

nonviolent resistance as a strategic weapon rather than merely a moral restraint that narrows their sphere of action.

Contents of this Monograph

The introduction of this monograph will contextualize the Tibetan nonviolent struggle for self-determination, putting forth a number of questions that the study will address. Chapter 1 will cover the existing literature on Tibetan nonviolent resistance, noting that the narrative of Tibetan history, at best, de-emphasizes nonviolent resistance, and at worst, ignores it entirely. This chapter also outlines the key arguments in the monograph. Chapter 2 will provide historical background on Tibet and the events leading up to China's invasion in 1959. Policies of isolation and disarmament, as well as religious and sectarian divisions in the Tibetan community, superseded national interests and undermined the ability of the Tibetan state as a whole to resist Chinese invasion and occupation.

Chapter 3 will discuss the first Tibetan uprising, the beginning and end of the Tibetan guerrilla resistance, and the seeds of nonviolent resistance planted at the time. It will note how nonviolent resistance played a peripheral role, while armed rebellions took center stage. Chapter 4 will discuss the period between the first and second uprisings, mainly focusing on the 1980s during which the Tibetan leadership in exile pursued a new strategy of "internationalization." In parallel, Tibetans in Tibet underwent an era of cultural revival amid Deng Xiaoping's policy of "liberalization." Chapter 5 will analyze the second Tibetan uprising, which took place from 1987 to 1989 (but did not die out until 1993). In this uprising, the protests exhibited a high degree of nonviolent discipline when led by monks and nuns, but the discipline quickly disappeared when the circle of participants expanded to include lay Tibetans. It will also discuss the various nonviolent tactics used by Tibetans during this period, and the transition from violent to nonviolent resistance.

Chapter 6 will focus on the 1990s when the global grassroots movement for Tibet gathered momentum and reached its peak. This chapter will study the factors that led to the rise of this global advocacy movement, and eventually its decline. Chapter 7 will discuss the third Tibetan uprising that began in 2008, the conditions that led to it

and the evolution of the resistance following the uprising. It will examine the elements of cultural renaissance, economic growth and social mobilization in the years leading up to 2008, which constituted a period of cultural preparation for this uprising. It will also study the aftermath of the event, including the Lhakar movement and how it is transforming the resistance still today.

Chapter 8 will provide a comparative analysis of nonviolent tactics used in the three uprisings, and explore the disconnect between the overall strategy of the Tibetan leadership and the organic planning of the Tibetan grassroots. This chapter will consider the kinds of tactics — protest and persuasion, noncooperation and intervention — that have been most popular and widely used in the movement.

This categorization of nonviolent tactics into three broad classes is borrowed from Gene Sharp.

Chapter 9 will offer concluding thoughts on the strategic challenges of Tibetan nonviolent resistance, developing the idea that Tibetans are now engaging in 'transformative resistance' — a sophisticated struggle which focuses on mind, speech and action to work towards liberation from the colonized mindset.

In Chapter 10, the monograph concludes by offering recommendations for Tibetan leadership and external actors to consider to increase the struggle's chances of success.

Key Arguments

1. Contrary to some views that the Tibetan movement has radicalized, it has in fact moved away from violence since the 1950s. The first uprising (1956-59) was largely violent, comprised of numerous armed rebellions. The second uprising (1987-89) was largely nonviolent, but confined to Lhasa. The third uprising (2008) was largely nonviolent and spread to all three historical provinces of Tibet.

2. The principled approach to nonviolent resistance grounded in Buddhism was the dominant framework in which the Tibetan leadership has considered the struggle. However, among the Tibetan grassroots this approach is being replaced by a more

Chapter 1: Literature Review

strategic conceptualization of the struggle that views nonviolent action as a weapon rather than an ideal.

3. Gene Sharp developed a theoretical model by which he explains four mechanisms that change the relationship between a nonviolent movement and its opponent: conversion, accommodation, persuasion and disintegration.[10, 11] The Tibetan leadership has pursued a strategy that relies heavily on building international diplomatic pressure on China, aimed at achieving change for Tibet through some form of conversion of Chinese political elites rather than nonviolent coercion or disintegration of the occupying regime. But to increase their chances of success, Tibetans must recalibrate their strategy in the form of a plan that harnesses not only international but also domestic power of social, economic and political organizing and institution building. Through mobilization of these forces, Tibetans can increase the pressure on China, which is the only viable way to move a regime that has proven highly unlikely to accommodate or be persuaded.

4. A nonviolent political uprising is often preceded by periods of cultural preparation during which a society's capacity for mobilization and its organizing networks become stronger.[12] Both the second and third uprisings were preceded by eras of cultural renaissance that emboldened the people and created greater capacity for them to seek political freedom through collective action.

5. In many resistance discourses, culture is portrayed as a fragile asset that needs to be shielded by political struggle, but rarely as a sword with which to pursue political change. The Tibetan resistance movement, for example, was long dominated by a fear-driven discourse that stressed the importance of "preserving" and "protecting" Tibetan culture from the onslaught of assimilation and modernity. Such narratives gave rise to the idea of culture as a beautiful but fragile flower that cannot protect itself. But in recent years, Tibetans have embraced a more confident and open-minded conception of culture, and have begun to tap into their unique language and literary traditions, religious systems, poetry and music as resistance tools to fight for political change.[13]

6. Despite being largely unknown to the rest of the world, Tibetans today are

---

[11] Srdja Popovic, Hardy Merriman, and Ivan Marovic et. al, *Canvas Core Curriculum: A Guide to Effective Nonviolent Struggle* (Belgrade: Center for Applied Nonviolent Action and Strategies, 2007).

[12] The independence struggle in India and the struggle to forge the Polish nation were preceded by periods of cultural renaissance.

[13] Tenzin Dorjee, "Why Lhakar Matters: The Elements of Tibetan Freedom," in *Tibetan Political Review*, 10 January 2013, http://www.tibetanpoliticalreview.org/articles/whylhakarmatterstheelementsoftibetanfreedom.

engaging in a growing noncooperation movement. Since the 2008 uprising erupted across Tibet, China's militarization of the Tibetan plateau has snuffed out all signs of dissent in the streets. But the revolution did not disappear; it simply moved indoors. Tibetans are engaged in a movement to speak only in Tibetan, to eat only in Tibetan restaurants, or to buy only from Tibetan shops. Tibetans are channeling their spirit of resistance into social, cultural and economic activities that are noncooperative (refusing to support Chinese institutions and businesses) and self-constructive (promoting Tibetan language and culture) which constitute the basis of what this monograph later refers to as 'transformative resistance.' The creative resistance efforts are helping to strengthen Tibetan national fabric against China's denationalization policies in Tibet.

7. The fact that Tibetans are waging a quiet, slow-building nonviolent movement in the most repressive political climate shows that there is a way to mobilize people power against the Chinese regime through lower-risk yet still powerful resistance actions.

8. The first uprising (1956-59) was a direct response to China's attack on religion through the implementation of "democratic reforms" in Tibet, and thus a reactive uprising in which religion was the epicenter of mobilization. The second (1987-89) was a pro-active campaign in the sense that the central theme was political, and the overriding demand was independence. The third uprising (2008) was also more proactive in nature as it revolved around several demands that included calls for the return of the Dalai Lama, freedom and independence for Tibet, democracy and solidarity. During the period that followed, culture became a rallying point for Tibetans, moving the nonviolent resistance beyond disruptive actions and more toward constructive means of the generational struggle against the Chinese-enforced status quo. These strategies are more inward-looking as they focus first of all on strengthening the Tibetan cultural, social and economic fabric to better prepare the Tibetan nation to fend off the Chinese policies of de-Tibetanization.

9. One of the key features of the Tibetan struggle has been a strong reliance on external actors, especially for financial assistance and political support. The nonviolent nature of the resistance after the 1987 uprising enabled the Tibetans to win over the global public opinion to an extent that would have been impossible through armed struggle. However, as a nonviolent grassroots struggle, the movement's greatest strength is its own bottom-up force, and no amount of external aid can match or substitute for this. Tibetans must recognize the limits of international support, and focus on strengthening their domestic mobilization.

Chapter 2
Historical Background

Ancient Tibet

Tibet, which is about four times the size of continental France, is located between the two most populous nations on earth: India and China. Traditionally inhabited exclusively by Tibetans, today the Chinese population in Tibet outnumbers the roughly 6 million Tibetans.[14] According to a groundbreaking 2014 study published by the University of Chicago and Case Western Reserve University, the first prototypal Tibetans settled on the Tibetan plateau some 30,000 years ago.[15] The study concluded that a particular gene inherited from a certain cousin of Neanderthals, known as Denisovans, helped the Tibetans adapt to high-altitude life, allowing them to survive in a harsh environment where others would have perished.

The Tibetan empire rose in the 6th century and reached its apex as a regional military power in the 8th century (see Figure 2). Its reputation in those days was a far cry from today's pacifist image of meditating Buddhist monks invoked by the very mention of the word "Tibet." At its height, the Tibetan empire's sphere of control included territories in modern day Bhutan, Sikkim, north Afghanistan, north India and north Nepal. Tibetans collected tributes from neighboring states including China. In 763, when the Chinese emperors of the Tang dynasty stopped paying tribute to Tibet, the Tibetans invaded the Chinese capital and occupied it for 15 days. This incident, one of the earliest recorded chapters of hostility between the two nations, ended with the signing of the Sino-Tibetan

---

[14] Tibetans claim that there are 7.5 million Chinese in Tibet today compared to the 6 million Tibetans. Established by the Chinese in 1965, the Tibet Autonomous Region, which represents approximately half of Tibet and where slightly less than half of the Tibetan population resides, is the only region in Tibet where the Chinese population is smaller than the Tibetan. In Amdo (Qinghai) and Kham (Sichuan) Chinese settlers have overtaken the number of Tibetans. To read more on the origin of Tibet, see W. D. Shakabpa's *Tibet: A Political History*.

[15] Emilia Huerta-Sánchez et al. "Altitude adaptation in Tibetans caused by introgression of Denisovan-like DNA," in *Nature* 512, (14 August 2014), 194–197.

[16] Christopher Beckwith, *The Tibetans in the Ordos and North China: Considerations on the Role of the Tibetan Empire in World History*, 5.

Figure 2. Map of Tibetan Empire, circa 800 AD

Source: Via Wikimedia Commons,
https://commons.wikimedia.org/wiki/File:Tibetan_empire_greatest_extent_780s-790s_CE.png.

treaty of 821.[16]

Following the Tibetan rulers' embrace of Buddhism in the 9th century, Tibet underwent a unique political transformation — a voluntary process of disarmament. Tibet's military power steadily declined while the number of monks and monasteries skyrocketed. Instead of the imperialist powerhouse that it had been in the 7th and 8th centuries, Tibet became the epicenter of faith and learning in central Asia, attracting students and teachers from Mongolia, India and Nepal. Tibet no longer harassed or conquered its neighboring kingdoms. Its hard power was replaced by a soft power derived from its investment in Buddhism as the state religion. Tibet's decline as a military empire was hastened by the politically motivated assassinations

Chapter 2: Historical Background

of the 41st and 42nd kings, after which Tibet entered an era of fragmentation.

By the time the Mongols rose to global power, the Tibetan empire had shattered into numerous feuding kingdoms and chiefdoms.[17] The Tibetans voluntarily surrendered to Genghis Khan by offering him tribute, preempting an outright invasion. During the rise of Kublai Khan, the grandson of Genghis Khan and founder of the Yuan dynasty, Kublai developed a close relationship with the Tibetan lama Phagpa, who became the khan's spiritual tutor. Kublai gave Phagpa supreme authority over Tibet, launching the priest-patron relationship that defined Tibet's complicated relationship with the Mongols.[18] Under this arrangement, Tibetan lamas provided spiritual guidance to the Mongol khans and the khans supplied military protection to Tibet. Although this relationship saved the Tibetans temporarily from the brutality of direct Mongol rule, it lulled Tibetan leaders into a political slumber, causing them to squander state-building opportunities after the end of Mongol rule.

According to the Chinese government, China's political claim over Tibet dates back to the Yuan dynasty.[19] Beijing argues that Tibet became a part of China during its annexation by Kublai Khan, the Mongol emperor of China in the 13th century. Tibetans maintain that even at the height of Mongol power, Tibet was administered as a separate entity by Tibetan rulers while China was ruled directly as an integral part of the Mongol empire. Besides, when the Yuan dynasty collapsed, Tibet regained independence under the leadership of a new Tibetan ruler, Phagmodrupa Changchub Gyaltsen of the Kagyu sect of Tibetan Buddhism.[20] In 1358, all of central Tibet was brought under his rule as an independent nation, one full decade before China became independent.[21]

Around this time a new Buddhist sect called Geluk emerged. As the Geluk tradition grew more popular, its followers were persecuted by the Kagyu-supporting Tibetan king.

---

[17] The fragmentation of the Tibetan empire began after the assassination of Tibet's 42nd king Lhasay Dharma, known as Lang Dharma, whose two sons battled for power and split the royal court into factions.
[18] W.D. Shakabpa, *Tibet: A Political History* (New York: Potala Publications, 1984), 70.
[19] Elliot Sperling, *The China-Tibet Conflict: History and Polemics*, 10.
[20] After consolidating his rule over Tibet, Changchub Gyaltsen reorganized the administrative divisions of the state, eliminating the Mongol-style myriarchies in favor of numerous districts known as dzongs. Tibet historian W.D. Shakabpa writes in *Tibet: A Political History*: "He posted officials and guards at various places along the border with China and concentrated troops at the important centers in Tibet. The land was divided equally among the agriculturalists, and it was [stipulated] that one-sixth of the crops were to be taken as tax by the administration... During the reign of the Sakya lamas, suspected criminals had been executed summarily without a hearing, according to the custom of the Mongols. Changchub adopted the practice of the early religious kings of Tibet and devised 13 kinds of punishment, varying in severity according to the seriousness of the crime." The fact that Changchub Gyaltsen was able to administer Tibet as its unquestioned sovereign further proves that Yuan control over Tibet had vanished with the fall of the Sakyas.
[21] Morris Rossabi, *China Among Equals* (Berkeley: University of California Press, 1983), 194.

But the Gelukpa acquired the backing of a powerful Mongol warrior named Gushri Khan. The Mongols killed the Kagyu king and crowned the Fifth Dalai Lama, the head of the Geluk tradition, as the supreme authority over all of Tibet in 1642.[22] Thus began three and a half centuries of Dalai Lama rule. However, many of the Dalai Lamas died too young to rule, so real political power was exercised by a series of regents. The reincarnation system[23] — while highly effective as a means of enabling religious institutions to preserve a lama's spiritual capital beyond his lifespan — turned out to be disastrous when applied to political succession. Each Dalai Lama's death was followed by a long interregnum during which Tibet suffered from a leadership vacuum, becoming vulnerable to foreign interference and civil war.

In 1720, the Manchus, descendants of the Jurchen people who had conquered China, launched an invasion of Tibet. This opened a new kind of priest-patron relationship in Tibet in which the Manchus had the upper hand. The Manchu emperor appointed two officials known as ambans to monitor the Tibetan rulers.[24] But during the mid-19th century, as the Manchus faced internal problems, their influence over Tibet waned. Soon, the strong-willed Thirteenth Dalai Lama erased the last remnants of Manchu control over Lhasa when, in 1897, he appointed his own top officials without consulting the ambans. By the dawn of the 20th century, Tibet enjoyed de facto independence.

This fragile stability was shattered in 1904 when Tibet was invaded by a British military expedition led by Colonel Younghusband.[25] The invasion, which did not have London's approval, prompted outrage from the British government[26] and Younghusband's forces quickly left.[27] In 1910, just a few years after the British left, Manchu troops invaded Tibet. Fortunately for Tibet, the Manchu dynasty collapsed two years later.[28] The Tibetans expelled the Manchus, first from central Tibet, and later from parts of eastern Tibet. On

---

[22] Samten Karmay, The Great Fifth, IIAS Newsletter #39.

[23] The institution of the reincarnated lamas was introduced by the Karmapa in the 13th century, and the practice was quickly adopted by other lamas. The genius of the reincarnation system was that it allowed the religious institution to preserve the charisma and influence of the lama beyond his lifetime. The devotees' faith in the lama — who never really dies but simply changes bodies as one changes clothes — accumulates across lifetimes. This explains the deep and enduring connection Tibetans generally feel with the Dalai Lama, whose relationship with the Tibetan public dates back to 1642, when the Fifth Dalai Lama assumed political power. However, the flip side of this advantage is that in between the passing of one Dalai Lama and the coming of the next, there is an interregnum during which the nation remains leaderless and vulnerable to foreign interference.

[24] Sam van Schaik, Tibet: A History (New Haven: Yale University Press, 2011), 143.

[25] Jamyang Norbu, Shadow Tibet: Selected Writings 1989-2004 (High Asia Press, 2007).

[26] Shakabpa, Tibet: A Political History, 219.

[27] Ibid., 217.

[28] Melvyn Goldstein, The Snow Lion and the Dragon: Tibet and the Dalai Lama (Berkeley: University of California Press, 1997), 30.

February 13, 1913, the Thirteenth Dalai Lama issued a five-point public statement reasserting Tibet's independence. The same year, Tibet and Mongolia signed a treaty recognizing each other's sovereignty.[29] From 1913 to 1949, Tibet once again became a de facto independent state, with no political influence from Mongol, Manchu or British forces.

The Thirteenth Dalai Lama's historic "Proclamation of Independence" marked the birth of the modern Tibetan state. In a bid to end Tibet's centuries-old isolationist policy, he introduced political, administrative and social reforms. He promoted secular education, modernized the army and reduced the power of the clergy. But he faced harsh opposition from the orthodox monastic authorities whose influence in the Tibetan government ran deep.[30] Despite the Thirteenth Dalai Lama's warning, Tibetans continued to rely on political isolation to protect their nation from external threats. In the 1920s, Tibetan leaders considered joining the League of Nations, but eventually decided against it after opposition from monastic conservatives. In hindsight, this isolationist policy made Tibet more vulnerable to foreign aggression. Tibetans' failure to join the League of Nations, and later the United Nations (UN), would come to haunt them for generations, although it is questionable whether even a UN membership could have truly protected Tibet from Chinese invasion at this point.

Chinese Invasion

In October 1949, the Chinese Communist Party came to power in China. Within a year, Mao Zedong launched the invasion of Tibet, and Chinese troops began advancing into eastern Tibet. The Tibetan army, made up of a few thousand soldiers, did not stand a chance against the better-armed Chinese force of 40,000 troops. Tibet's last hope was to appeal to the outside world for help. On November 7, 1950, Lhasa sent a frantic appeal to the UN for help. But two major factors made UN intervention unlikely. First, neither Tibet nor China was a member state of the newly formed international body. Second, none of the major powers of the time were willing to sponsor a discussion on Tibet in the General Assembly; Tibet was such an obscure place – geographically,

---

[29] Tashi Tsering, "The Tibeto-Mongol Treaty of January 1913" in *Lungta Journal* Issue 17, The Centennial of the Tibeto-Mongol Treaty: 1913-2013, Spring 2013.
[30] Van Schaik, *Tibet: A History*, 196.

economically and politically — that no one had a stake in it.[31] As it dawned on Lhasa that external intervention was impossible, it agreed to cooperate with the Chinese government's effort to consolidate control over Tibet. For the Tibetan leaders, it was either war or surrender; there was nothing in-between. Nonviolent resistance simply did not exist as an option in their repertoire of policy choices. Their neighbors to the south, the Indians had just gained their independence through a successful nonviolent movement, but the significance of this achievement was lost on the Tibetans.

On May 23, 1951, the Seventeen-Point Agreement[32] was signed between Tibetan and Chinese representatives, terminating Tibet's status as an independent state.[33] The agreement specified that Tibet's traditional social system would not be altered, that the position of the Dalai Lama would not be changed, and that China would exercise only symbolic power over Tibet. Many Tibetans, wrote the historian Tsering Shakya, believed that it mattered little if Tibet's legal status was surrendered to China as long as their social and cultural autonomy remained intact.[34] While Tibetan cultural and ethnic identities were strong, and clearly distinguished them from the Chinese, the Tibetan population's sense of political consciousness was relatively weak. The power of the Tibetan state was highly decentralized, and religious loyalty to regional monasteries surpassed political loyalty to Lhasa. In addition, Tibet's massive landmass, hostile terrain and lack of communications and transportation infrastructure made it even more challenging to develop a Tibetan political consciousness.

Soon after signing the "agreement," China waged a campaign to wipe out Tibetan Buddhist culture, destroying all but 12 of the nation's more than 6,000 monasteries.[35] Religious paintings, statues and other artifacts were destroyed, looted and melted in China's industrial furnaces. The Chinese banned traditional forms of Tibetan music, calling

---

[31] In the face of the military might that the Chinese had demonstrated, the Tibetan delegates felt that any resistance to signing the agreement would be futile. The Dalai Lama wrote that Ngabo Ngawang Jigme, the head of the delegation, signed the treaty to prevent further bloodshed from the continuation of the conflict. See Shakya, *The Dragon in the Land of Snows*, 52.

[32] To give its invasion of Tibet an appearance of legitimacy, China made Tibetan representatives sign the Seventeen-Point Agreement in 1951, which stipulated that the Tibetan people "shall unite and drive out imperialist aggressive forces from Tibet" and that the Tibetan people "shall return to the big family of the Motherland the People's Republic of China." It also provided that the Dalai Lama's powers and the traditional political and economic systems of Tibet would not be altered. Tibetans later repudiated what they saw as an unequal treaty signed under duress, arguing that the Tibetan delegates were not authorized to sign such a document in the first place.

[32] Ibid, 90.

[34] Ibid.

[35] Frank Moraes, *Revolt in Tibet* (New York: The Macmillan Company, 1960).

them antiquated and backward. Traditional genres of religious music such as *shon* in western Tibet, *gar* in Amdo, *dro drodung* and *kordro* in Kham were annihilated.[36] New genres of revolutionary folksongs and spoken drama were used as vehicles to disseminate communist propaganda, and included lyrics that likened Mao to "the rising sun in the east."

While the Chinese attack on the Buddhist order antagonized every section of Tibetan society, it eventually strengthened pan-Tibetan identity by generating a nationwide sense of victimhood. This was the outcome of backfire, whereby the state's violence against unarmed civilians produced the opposite of the intended result. China's use of violence against Tibetan civilians and religious figures offended the most deeply held Tibetan beliefs and values, pushing the Tibetans over the edge and forcing them to retaliate. Tibetans' hatred of the Chinese grew to the point that it overshadowed all the regional or sectarian differences that used to divide the Tibetans. United by their grievances, the Tibetans came to recognize that their only hope was a collective stand against China. A new sense of Tibetan national identity was born, and it would soon become the basis for political mobilization.

Buddhism, Nonviolence and Gandhi

Although many have come to view nonviolence as synonymous with Tibet, nonviolent resistance is a relatively new phenomenon in Tibetan culture. It is only in the last few decades, largely due to the Dalai Lama's influence, that nonviolence became a chief marker of Tibetan Buddhist identity.[37] In the past, nonviolence, though important in Buddhism, was not perceived as the hallmark of the religion.[38] Tibetans treated nonviolence and resistance as two incompatible variables: nonviolence implied submission, inaction and the omission of harm; resistance implied defiance, action and usually, violence. In the Tibetan psyche, nonviolence was a concept that applied to individual action in the moral dimension rather than collective action in the sociopolitical dimension. Buddhism, which played a greater role than any other philosophy or ideology in shaping the Tibetan worldview, has a history of existing side by side with

---
[36] Anna Morcom, *Unity and Discord: Music and Politics in Contemporary Tibet* (Tibet Information Network, 2004), 32.
[37] See page 10 for definitions of the terms "nonviolence" and "nonviolent action."
[38] Elliot Sperling, "Orientalism and Aspects of Violence in the Tibetan Tradition," in *Imagining Tibet: Perceptions, Projections and Fantasies*, ed. Dodin and Rather (Wisdom Publications, 2001), 319.

violence. "Kindness and compassion toward sentient beings," writes Elliot Sperling, "are a significant part of Tibetan Buddhism, as is, of course, the idea of working for the benefit of sentient beings. These are not, however, identical with Gandhian *ahimsa*; nor are they all there is to Tibetan Buddhism in practice." More important than *ahimsa* was the notion of protecting the Buddhist doctrine, by nonviolent means when possible, and violent means when necessary.[39]

Even by the middle of the 20th century, Tibetans showed little interest in the potential of – and the need for – nonviolent resistance. In 1944, when a Tibetan delegation attending the Afro-Asian Conference in Delhi offered a *khata*, a traditional white scarf, to Gandhi, he asked if it was a Tibetan-made product. Upon learning that the scarf was manufactured in China, Gandhi refused to accept it, insisting that he would prefer something produced by Tibetans themselves. Gandhi's experience with Indian self-reliance and economic noncooperation against the British must have prompted him to reject a Chinese-made Tibetan gift. In hindsight, Gandhi's message, tacitly invoking the connection between economic self-reliance and political independence, was nothing short of prophetic. But in 1944, since Tibet was still an independent country, this subtle message was probably lost on the Tibetan delegates at the conference.[40]

The only person to whom Gandhi's idea of nonviolence held some interest was the young Dalai Lama. In 1956, when he visited India for the 2,500th anniversary of the Buddha's birth, the 21-year-old Dalai Lama stood at the site of Gandhi's cremation and made a pledge to nonviolence. "As I stood there, I wondered what wise council the Mahatma would have given me if he had been alive," wrote the Dalai Lama years later in his autobiography. "I felt sure he would have thrown all his strength of will and character into a peaceful campaign for the freedom of the people of Tibet … I made up my mind … to follow his lead whatever difficulties might confront me. I determined more strongly than ever that I could never associate myself with acts of violence."[41] Although he was able to meet the Mahatma only in spirit, this moment would leave a lasting imprint on the Dalai Lama's life, and by extension, on Tibet's future. At the time, however, the Dalai Lama was too young to exercise leadership in Tibetan politics.

---

[39] Ibid.
[40] Nevertheless, more than a decade later, in 1958, the founding members of Chushi Gangdruk designed a logo featuring the Tibetan traditional sword as a symbol of Tibetan strength, self-reliance and resourcefulness.
[41] The Dalai Lama, *My Land and My People* (New York: Potala Publications, 1962).

Chapter 3
The First Tibetan Uprising (1956-59)

Armed Rebellion in Eastern Tibet in 1956

In mainstream Tibetan discourse, the first uprising is seen as an event confined to 1959, the year Tibetans in Lhasa revolted against Chinese occupation and the Dalai Lama fled into exile. However, the 1959 Lhasa rebellion was preceded by numerous incidents of armed uprising in eastern Tibet, although these uprisings have been overlooked in the Lhasa-centric documentation and telling of Tibetan history.[42] In 1956, the Chinese launched the notorious "democratic reforms" in Kham, southeastern Tibet, and Amdo, northeastern Tibet. Imposing communist ideology on Tibetans, China waged an anti-religion campaign targeting spiritual figures, monastic institutions, cultural practices and places of worship. These hostile measures – mass arrests, executions of religious leaders, the banning of rituals – sparked a violent rebellion known as the Khampa uprising. The revolt, which spread across eastern Tibet, temporarily managed to expel the Chinese from the region. But the Chinese army returned in greater numbers, and the Tibetan fighters retreated toward central Tibet, where the "democratic reforms" had not yet been implemented.

The rebellion of 1956 revolved around the idea of protecting religion. Named "The Volunteer Army to Defend Buddhism," the alliance invoked the protection of the Buddhist doctrine rather than the defense of the Tibetan nation. Political divisions along regional lines ran deep, and religion was the only cause that provided a unity of purpose around which people could mobilize on a national scale. Religion thus became the epicenter of Tibetan resistance in this period.

The leaders of the Khampa uprising, who had retreated from eastern to central

---

[42] For more information on the Lhasa-centric approach in the telling of Tibetan history, see Carole McGranhan, *Arrested Histories: Tibet, the CIA, and Memories of a Forgotten War* (Durham: Duke University Press, 2010).

Tibet, decided to reorganize their loosely knit alliance into a single resistance army. On June 16, 1958, they launched the Chushi Gangdruk armed resistance force under the leadership of Gonpo Tashi, a Khampa merchant-turned-warrior.[43] The resistance leaders approached several countries for military aid, but without success. Eventually, in one of the strangest partnerships of the Cold War, the CIA agreed to provide covert assistance to the Tibetans. Over the course of five years between 1959 and 1964, the CIA trained 259 Tibetans in guerrilla warfare at Camp Hale in Colorado.[44]

1959 Lhasa Uprising

At the height of the Khampa uprising, Mao Zedong was receiving daily briefs on Tibet. In a situation report for top Chinese leaders, the Xinhua News Agency warned that the revolts in eastern Tibet "have gathered pace and developed into a nearly full-scale rebellion."[45] But Mao, unperturbed by the outbreak of violence, responded:

> In the Tibetan area over the next several years, the enemy side and our side will compete for the [support of the] masses and test the ability of the armed forces. After several years — for example, three to four years, or five to six years, or seven to eight years—it is inevitable that a great showdown will occur. Only then can the problems be thoroughly resolved. Initially, the military forces deployed by the Tibetan rulers were quite weak, but now they command a rebel force of 10,000 whose combat spirit is relatively high. This is a dangerous enemy for us. But this is not necessarily a bad thing; rather, it could be a good thing because it enables [us] to resolve the problem through war.[46]

It is easy to see why Mao wanted to resolve the Tibet problem through war. The Chinese clearly enjoyed the advantage of a larger troop size, superior arms, better communications technology and infrastructure. "As soon as you choose to fight with violence," argues Sharp, "you're choosing to fight against your opponent's best weapons."[47]

---

[43] Ibid, 2.
[44] Tenzing Sonam and Ritu Sarin, *Shadow Circus: The CIA in Tibet*.
[45] Chen Jian, "The Tibetan Rebellion of 1959 and China's Changing Relations with India and the Soviet Union," in the *Journal of Cold War Studies*, Volume 8 Issue 3 Summer 2006, Cold War Studies at Harvard University.
[46] Ibid.
[47] Ruaridh Arrow, "Gene Sharp: Author of the nonviolent revolution rulebook," *BBC News*, 21 February 2011, http://www.bbc.co.uk/news/world-middle-east-12522848.

Chapter 3: The First Tibetan Uprising (1956-59)

Mao thus viewed the potential crisis as a timely excuse to justify introducing "democratic reforms" in central Tibet with the full force of war.[48]

In early March 1959, a rumor spread through Lhasa that the Dalai Lama had been invited to an opera at the Chinese military camp, and was told to come alone. Tibetans saw this as China's attempt to kidnap the Dalai Lama. The news spread like wildfire, thanks to a monk who rode his horse around the city telling people to gather at the Norbulingka the next day, in an act reminiscent of Paul Revere's 'midnight ride' to alert the colonial militia of the approaching British forces in 1775.[49] In a matter of hours ordinary Tibetans from all over Lhasa surrounded the Norbulingka, the Dalai Lama's summer palace. The crowd was united by the common purpose of protecting the Dalai Lama's life, and their tactic was to surround his palace so that no Chinese could enter it. In what was one of the first recorded uses of a nonviolent intervention tactic in Tibet, the people used their bodies as human shields.

> *In the absence of planning or clear leadership, what started as a peaceful gathering spiraled into chaos...*

However, in the absence of planning or clear leadership, what started as a peaceful gathering spiraled into chaos, as the crowd vented their grievances at Tibetan officials who had collaborated with the Chinese. One of these officials, Khunchung Sonam Gyamtso, arrived at the Norbulingka wearing monastic robes and entered the palace, but came out in a white shirt, dark pants and a Chinese cap. Enraged that he had abandoned traditional clothes for Chinese attire, the crowd beat Kunchung to death.[50] This violent turn of events was in part due to weak or non-existent leadership and a lack of strategy; these elements arguably could have helped prevent the crowd from turning into an unruly mob.

On March 11, 1959, thousands of people showed up in Shol village, situated at the foot of the Potala Palace, in the largest demonstration ever staged in Lhasa. A meeting was held during which 50 government officials set up a new group, called the People's Assembly, in defiance of China's meddling in the government in Lhasa.[51] This constituted

---

[48] Jian, *The Tibetan Rebellion of 1959*.
[49] David Hackett Fischer, *Paul Revere's Ride*, 1995.
[50] Shan, Chao, "Sunshine after Rain," in *Peking Review*, 5 May 1950, 10.
[51] Kalimpong Correspondent of the *Times of India*, "A Traitor Stoned to Death," Bombay, 17 April 1959, in *Tibet Fights for Freedom*, 1960.

the classic nonviolent act of rejecting a political authority by setting up an alternative one. The speakers who addressed the crowd condemned the Chinese and called the masses to mobilize to overthrow Chinese rule. The People's Assembly repudiated the Seventeen-Point Agreement. On March 12, the crowd marched toward the two foreign missions in Lhasa, the Indian and Nepalese missions, and called for the Indians and Nepalese to support Tibetan independence.[52] Surprisingly, in a complete departure from its policy of appeasing the Chinese, the Tibetan government authorized the distribution of arms from its arsenals to the Tibetan public.[53]

Text continued

---

[52] Appeal to Indian Consul, New Delhi, Speech by Mr. Nehru in the Lok Sabha, on 4 May 1959.
[53] Tibet Information Network, *A Struggle of Blood and Fire: The Imposition of Martial Law in 1989 and the Lhasa Uprising in 1959* (1999).

Chapter 3: The First Tibetan Uprising (1956-59)

Figure 3. Map of Tibetan Plateau with International and Disputed Boundaries

Source: Treasury of Lives, Rubin Foundation. A high-resolution version of this map can be downloaded at: http://treasuryoflives.org/maps/up main_map/main_map.pdf.

Chapter 3: The First Tibetan Uprising (1956-59)

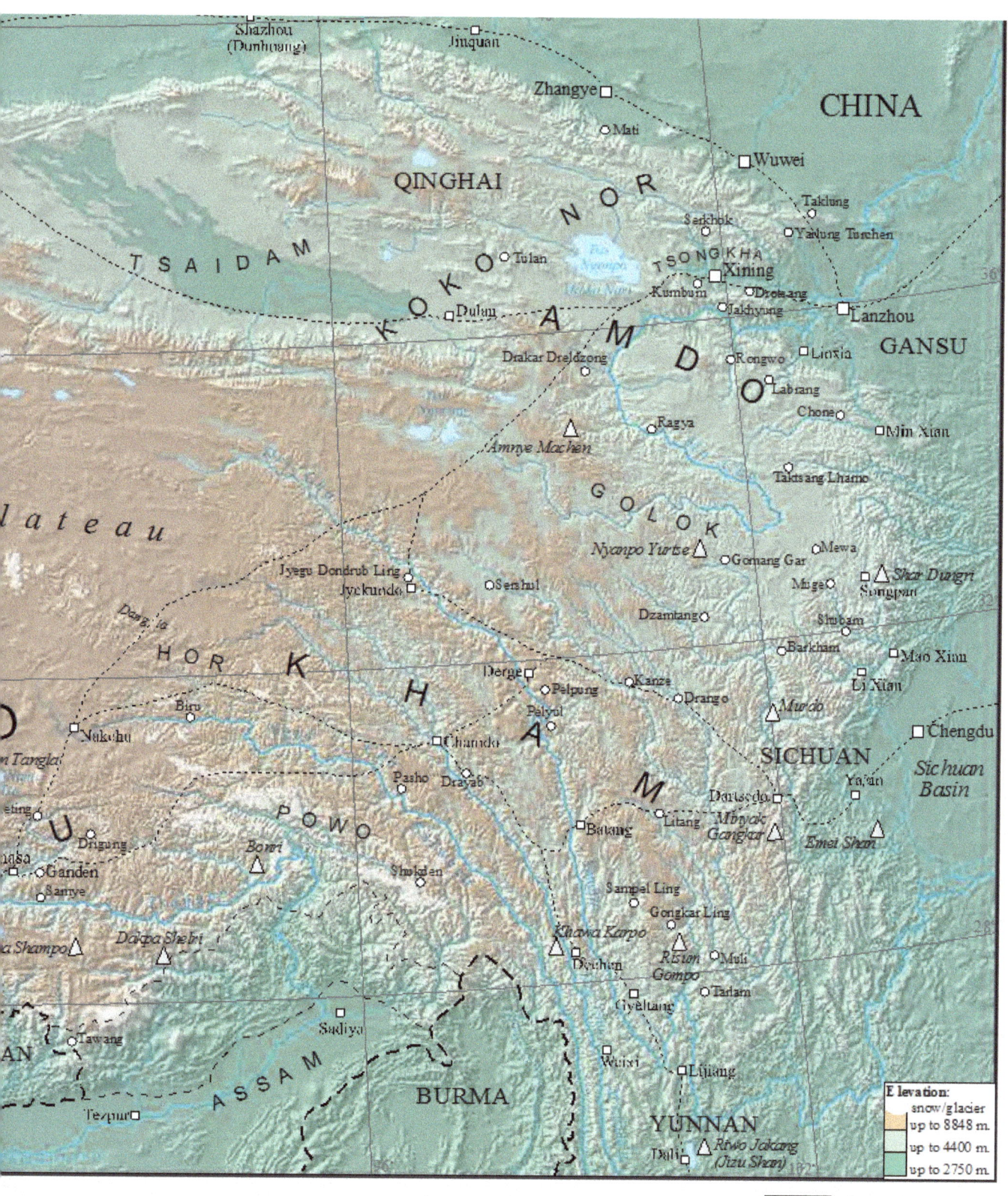

For a week, the demonstrators ruled the city. The revolt was spreading to other regions of Tibet like Gyantse and Phari, and news of the revolt was trickling to the outside world (see Figure 3). On March 17, as the Chinese shelled parts of Lhasa to intimidate the demonstrators, the Dalai Lama fled Lhasa. On March 19, Tibetan rebels started attacking Chinese administrative and military targets.[54] The next day, the Chinese launched a massive counteroffensive to quell the revolt. According to the Chinese government's count, 87,000 Tibetans were killed in the uprising.[55] The Tibetan government estimates that 430,000 Tibetans died during the uprising, and 260,000 Tibetans died in prisons and labor camps from 1950 to 1984.[56] All in all, if one takes into account the years leading up to the 1959 uprising and the tumultuous decades since, it is believed that over a million Tibetans died as a direct result of China's invasion and occupation. The International Commission of Jurists (ICJ) wrote in its 1959 and 1960 reports that the Chinese government had committed many "acts of genocide" against the Tibetan people.[57]

Despite the fact that during this period Tibetans used 22 types of nonviolent tactics (see Figure 5 in Chapter 8), the movement remained by and large violent from 1956 to 1959. Perhaps the most significant nonviolent action of the Tibetan government during this period was to establish the Tibetan government in exile, a parallel institution that would continue to command the loyalty of the Tibetan people. This exile government would serve three important roles:

1. It became the main welfare institution providing many kinds of services (health, education, financial, etc.) to the growing number of Tibetan refugees;
2. It was also a political institution that gave legitimacy to the Tibetan struggle and remained a source of unity for Tibetans both in Tibet and outside; and
3. It became the sole representative of the Tibetan people in interactions with international bodies and foreign governments, firstly the Indian government and subsequently other governments.

A sign of its success is that even to this day, Tibetans living in every continent pay a

---

[54] Chen Jian, The Tibetan Rebellion of 1959 and China's Changing Relations with India and the Soviet Union, *Journal of Cold War Studies*, Volume 8 Issue 3 Summer 2006, Cold War Studies at Harvard University.
[55] Shakya, *Dragon in the Land of Snows*.
[56] "Tibet Fact Sheets, Key Facts on the Chinese Occupation," Official website of the Tibetan government in exile, accessed July 2014, http://www.tibet.com.
[57] ICJ Report on Tibet, 1960.

fixed "voluntary tax," known as the Greenbook Contribution, to the Tibetan government in exile, as practical support to the institution as well as a symbolic pledge of allegiance to the struggle.[58] It is estimated that roughly 40 percent of the Tibetan government's annual administrative budget is covered by the Greenbook Contributions from Tibetans across the world. For example, $230,970 was collected from North America alone between October 2013 and April 2014. This is an example of self-propelled financial organizing at the grassroots level.

The CIA's Tibet Connection

Amid the chaos that accompanied the Lhasa uprising of 1959, the Chushi Gangdruk fighters helped facilitate the Dalai Lama's escape from Tibet. After arriving in India, these militias continued their operations from a base in Mustang, Nepal in collaboration with the CIA. Although severely outnumbered and under-equipped, the Tibetan guerrillas achieved a few victories. The most significant achievement was that they successfully escorted the Dalai Lama to India. However, these modest victories came at a high cost. To this day, critics claim that the CIA's involvement in Tibet undermined the legitimacy of the Tibetan cause. In the lead up to the US-China rapprochement, the CIA stopped funding this operation in 1969. The Mustang base was subsequently shut down; it could not operate without external support.[59]

A weakness of armed resistance is that, unlike nonviolent struggles, it has to rely heavily on external support – arms, ammunition, supplies and cash. The question remains whether the espoused benefits of accepting US logistical assistance during the Cold War were worth the lingering moral and political costs as well as social stigma of having partnered with the CIA. Fortunately, Tibetans simultaneously engaged in institution-building and other nonviolent actions that outlived any armed organizing.

---

[58] Tibetan adults living in India, Bhutan and Nepal contribute 58 Indian rupees (about 1 USD in 2015) per year toward this 'voluntary tax' while Tibetans in other countries contribute USD 96 per year. The income from this revenue stream helps fund many programs of the Tibetan exile administration.

[59] Kenneth Knaus, *Orphans of the Cold War* (Public Affairs, 1999).

Renunciation of Violence

In 1974, the Dalai Lama sent a taped message to the Tibetan guerrillas in Mustang asking them to lay down their arms. As a Buddhist monk, the Dalai Lama had long expressed a principled opposition to violence, and felt deeply uncomfortable about the guerrilla operation. On top of that, as Beijing and Kathmandu grew closer, it became impossible for the Nepali government to turn a blind eye to the existence of Mustang. In Dharamsala's view, the political and moral liability of Mustang outweighed its strategic utility. So, nearly two decades after it began, the chapter of Tibetan armed struggle came to a close.

What followed was a decade of political limbo, an era when the direction of the struggle was shrouded in doubt. In fact, in the mid-1970s, the view from Dharamsala was bleak. China had completed its rapprochement with the United States and secured its re-entry into the UN. Geopolitically speaking, there was no major entity posing a serious challenge to the legitimacy of Chinese rule in Tibet.[60] In the eyes of Beijing, Tibetans in Tibet had been completely subdued, while those in exile had become irrelevant. The Tibet issue had all but disappeared, not only from the international political stage but also from global public consciousness.

---

[60] Robert Barnett, "Violated Specialness: Western Political Representations on Tibet" in *Imagining Tibet: Perceptions, Projections and Fantasies*, ed. Thierry Dodin and Heinz Rather (Boston: Wisdom Publications, 2001), 272.

Chapter 4
Internationalization in Exile, Liberalization in Tibet (1980s)

In Exile: A New Strategy to 'Internationalize' the Tibet Issue

In the 1980s, the Tibetan leadership developed a long-term nonviolent strategy for reinvigorating the Tibetan cause. Dharamsala decided to "internationalize" the Tibet issue, thereby expanding the domain of conflict beyond Tibet.[61] Instead of allowing its state of exile and lack of access to Tibet to become a liability, Dharamsala decided to use it to its advantage by choosing a new terrain for battle: the global political arena and the court of international public opinion. The crux of the strategy was to use the liberal democracies of the West to pressure Beijing into making concessions.[62] Rather than trying to appeal to the UN, an organization with little leverage over China, Dharamsala decided to direct its efforts toward the publics and the governments of democratic nations in the West, particularly the United States.[63]

This strategic recalibration in Dharamsala manifested itself in the rising frequency of the Dalai Lama's global tours. The Tibetan leader, who led a sedentary life in the first two decades of exile, suddenly became a jet-setter, flying from country to country with the goal of building international public support for Tibet. Between 1959 and 1985, the Dalai Lama had visited one country per year on average.[64] But between 1986 and 1999, he made 63 international trips, averaging nearly 10 countries in five trips per year.[65] He also began to meet with international dignitaries and world leaders with greater frequency during this period. Before 1985, he met with an average of three international

---

[61] Goldstein, *The Snow Lion and the Dragon*, 75. Goldstein mentions that the new strategy was finalized after a series of high-level meetings between key Tibetan and Western supporters in New York, Washington and London in 1986-87.
[62] Shakya, *The Dragon in the Land of Snows*, 413.
[63] Barnett, *Violated Specialness*, 273.
[64] Source of raw data for these figures is the Dalai Lama's official website: www.dalailama.com.
[65] Ibid.

dignitaries per year, but from 1986 to 1999 he met with 10 dignitaries each year.[66] The Dalai Lama's speaking tours set off an explosion of public awareness about Tibet's plight, galvanizing thousands of youth in the West to join the Tibet movement. Many of them became advocates for freedom and human rights in Tibet. Advocacy organizations such as the International Campaign for Tibet in Washington, DC, Students for a Free Tibet in New York, and the Free Tibet Campaign in London came into existence. Western students of Buddhism began to see the Tibetan struggle as a virtuous campaign to save a Buddhist culture from destruction, and channeled their spiritual commitment into political activism.

Dharamsala used its state of exile and lack of access to Tibet to its own advantage by choosing a new terrain for battle: the global political arena and the court of international public opinion.

However, Western recognition of the Tibetan struggle raised the pressure on the Dalai Lama to appear accommodating and reasonable. In the Strasbourg Proposal of 1988, he made a very detrimental compromise: he conceded Tibet's independence in favor of "genuine autonomy," meaning a high degree of autonomy in which Tibetans would control all of their affairs except foreign relations and defense. While many world leaders hailed this as a courageous compromise, it dismayed the Tibetans. In the eyes of activists demanding Tibetan independence, Dharamsala had squandered one of its most valuable bargaining chips – their historical claim to sovereignty – by preemptively surrendering independence. Not only did this unilateral concession fail to draw any reciprocal gesture from China, it also fractured the Tibetan sense of purpose that had sustained their morale until then.

In Tibet: A Period of Liberalization (1980-87)

Around the same time that Dharamsala launched its strategy of "internationalization," Tibetans in Tibet began to emerge from the shadow of Mao's tyranny. Tibet entered a period of liberalization under Deng Xiaoping, China's new paramount leader, who repealed many of the harsh Maoist policies. In May 1980, when

---

[66] Source of raw data for these figures is the Dalai Lama's official website: www.dalailama.com.

Chapter 4: Internationalization in Exile, Liberalization in Tibet (1980s)

Communist Party Secretary Hu Yaobang visited Tibet, his shock at the disastrous impact of Chinese rule on the Tibetan economy, culture and society led him to exclaim, "This reminds me of colonialism."[67] He laid down a new Tibet policy, emphasizing that, "Efforts should be made to revive and develop Tibetan culture, education and science."[68] Hu's visit resulted in reforms that represented "Beijing's attempt to redress the wrongs that had been done to Tibetans and in the process win their trust and support, albeit within the framework that Tibet was an inalienable part of China."[69] Most importantly, the Panchen Lama, Tibet's second most important religious leader, began traveling across Tibet, exhorting Tibetans to study their native language, practice their culture and revive their religion.

The Tibetans welcomed this new era of leniency under which China allowed them to observe religious rituals and cultural practices that had been strictly banned in the 1960s and 70s. Tibetans "once again wore traditional clothes, men grew their hair long and wore it in braids – fashions which had been banned and severely punished during the Cultural Revolution."[70] Religious practices were decriminalized – Tibetans started turning their prayer wheels, decorating altars in their homes, and circumambulating holy sites.[71] Communities in villages and towns launched grassroots efforts to resurrect monasteries and temples that had been ravaged in the frenzy of the Cultural Revolution.

As restrictions on expression were partially lifted, Tibetans began producing numerous works of art and literature – magazines, books, songs and paintings. Writers began to publish essays and books that glorified the Tibetan nation. Musicians collaborated with poets and composers to create songs with undercurrents of national resistance. In 1983, the poet Dhondup Gyal, founding father of modern Tibetan literature, wrote "Waterfall of Youth", which "caused a sensation when it was published, both for its radical literary innovation and bold nationalistic sentiments."[72] When another poem of his, a tribute to "Lake Kokonor" in Amdo, was rendered to music and performed by the pop star Dadon, it became the unofficial anthem for a new generation of Tibetans.

Among all the arts, music stood out as the predominant medium through which

---

[67] Ronald Schwartz, *Circle of Protest* (New York: Columbia University Press, 1994).
[68] Ibid, 16.
[69] Goldstein, *The Snow Lion and the Dragon*, 67.
[70] Schwartz, *Circle of Protest*, 16.
[71] Ibid. Circumambulation refers to the act of walking clockwise around a temple or other holy sites, a ritual believed by Buddhists to be a way of accumulating spiritual merit.
[72] Dechen Pempa, "Waterfall of Youth – Dhondup Gyal," *High Peaks Pure Earth*, 16 February 2011, http://highpeakspureearth.com/2011/waterfall-of-youth-dhondup-gyal-music-video-by-yudrug-green-dragon/.

ordinary Tibetans participated in the revival of culture, fostering a sense of national identity. There is an element of irony in this phenomenon: in the 1950s and 60s, it was Mao who wielded music as a tool of repression. The Chinese manipulated Tibetan operas, creating new versions that preached communist ideology instead of Buddhist teachings. A popular Maoist tactic was to appropriate Tibetan folk songs and replace the original lyrics with communist propaganda. The pro-Beijing Tibetan soprano, Tseten Dolma, was reviled by Tibetans for singing Mao's praise to the tune of timeless Tibetan folk songs. In a reversal of roles,

> *The small dose of cultural freedom sensitized the Tibetans to their lack of political freedom, and made them restless for greater change.*

when Tibetans embraced music as a major tool of resistance in the 1980s, many Tibetan singers appropriated popular Chinese melodies and inserted their own lyrics glorifying Tibet's independent history, the Dalai Lama, the Tibetan landscape and the resistance movement.[73]

The Tibetans' innate love of music is well known, but it was not the only reason music became such a popular tool of Tibetan resistance. Music allows those fighting oppression to occupy a gray area that is nonexistent in politics. Music provides an elasticity and malleability that make political resistance less incriminating — and repression against it even less justifiable. Singers like Jampa Tsering, Dadon and Palgon embraced music as a vehicle for invoking faith in the Dalai Lama, using metaphors such as "the sun," "uncle" or "white crane" to refer to him implicitly. The metaphors protected them; Tibetan listeners knew to whom the singers were referring to but the authorities usually did not (even if they did, it would have seemed absurd to censor songs that praised a bird).

Limited though they were, the new policies of the 1980s ushered in new channels of communication between the Tibetans in Tibet and those in exile. Tibetans were permitted to travel to Nepal and India to visit family members. Many used this opportunity to travel to Dharamsala and meet the Dalai Lama. In fact, Dharamsala became a political mecca for Tibetans. These pilgrims returned to Tibet with new hopes for freedom, regaling the teahouses in Lhasa with news of the Dalai Lama's growing popularity abroad. This

---

[73] Tibet in Song, a documentary film by Ngawang Choephel, 2010.

new line of trans-Himalayan communication emboldened the Tibetans. The Chinese leadership had thought that allowing modest religious and social freedoms would satisfy the Tibetans enough that they would forgo their more contentious desire for political freedom. But Beijing was wrong. Liberalization – like repression earlier – brought about the opposite effect. The small dose of cultural freedom sensitized the Tibetans to their lack of political freedom, and made them restless for greater change.

During this period of liberalization, around 1984, Chinese settlers started moving to Tibet in great numbers.[74] Beijing's plans to develop Tibet attracted tens of thousands of Chinese laborers and investors whose presence began changing the cultural, economic and demographic landscape of Tibet. In 1950, there were hardly any Chinese in central Tibet, whereas by 1988 there were approximately a million Chinese in the Tibet Autonomous Region alone. As more Tibetans lost their jobs and opportunities to Chinese settlers, their grievances against the system and the state intensified. While the liberalization of some policies gave Tibetans a new confidence to assert their identity, the policy of population transfer exacerbated their grievances against what they saw as a second invasion. This new manifestation of cultural unity heightened the collective sense of belonging among Tibetans. The fusion of all these forces reignited the dreams of a Tibetan nation-state.

Tibetans did not reach out to Chinese settlers during this period to explore areas of common grievances against the state. Tibetans saw themselves as victims not only of the Chinese state but also of Chinese settlers, whose interests – economic, cultural and political – seemed diametrically opposed to theirs. The fact that Tibetans and Chinese spoke different languages, ate different foods, ran in different social and religious circles, and pursued different life priorities meant there was very little ground on which a common cause was possible to find or build. As far as Tibetans were concerned, it was a zero-sum existential struggle between them and the Chinese settlers closely aligned with the Chinese state.

---

[74] Goldstein, *The Snow Lion and the Dragon*, 84.

Chapter 5
The Second Tibetan Uprising (1987-89)

The second Tibetan uprising was nonviolent and distinctly different from the first. The central theme of the discourse and epicenter of mobilization shifted from the religious realm to the political one. While the first uprising emphasized the defense of religion, the second one rallied around seeking political independence. Whereas the first uprising consisted of armed rebellions between 1956 and 1959, the second one manifested itself in a series of nonviolent demonstrations confined mostly to Lhasa between 1987 and 1989. Because using violence constituted a violation of the monastic law, during the first uprising monks gave up their vows and robes to pick up arms. In the second popular revolution, the nonviolent nature of the tactics allowed the monks not only to retain their vows but also to become leaders of the resistance.

Protests and Riots in Lhasa – 1987

In September 1987, the Dalai Lama paid a high-profile visit to Washington, DC to speak before a congressional caucus on human rights. Tibetans in Tibet ecstatically followed the news. On state television, Chinese leaders condemned the Dalai Lama for trying to "split the motherland." The harsh accusations levied against the Dalai Lama were meant to warn Tibetans not to support him. Tibetans, whose reverence for the Dalai Lama was undiminished even after three decades of separation, were enraged by China's invective against their leader.[75] The monks of the Drepung Monastery decided to defend the Dalai Lama's reputation by showing the world that Tibetans stood with him.

---
[75] Shakya, *Dragon in the Land of Snows*, 417.

On September 27, 21 monks from the Drepung Monastery, the largest institution of learning in Tibet, staged a demonstration in the center of Lhasa.[76] They opened the protest with a procession circumambulating the Jokhang, Tibet's holiest temple, waving a handmade version of the Tibetan national flag. They chanted "Independence for Tibet" and "May the Dalai Lama Live Ten Thousand Years." As they completed the first circle around the Jokhang, they were "spontaneously joined by 100 people."[77] After completing the third circle, they marched toward the regional administrative offices of the Chinese government, where the police violently broke up the demonstration and arrested participants.

This incident, "though relatively small, breathed new life into the Tibetan nonviolent movement."[78] It launched the birth of the modern Tibetan resistance movement, setting off a chain of protests that continued through 1993. Ironically, the catalyst of this protest was China. If China had not attacked the Dalai Lama publicly, the Drepung monks might not have felt the need to defend his reputation by marching in the streets. Perhaps Tibetans in Lhasa, whose only source of news was Chinese state television, might not have even known that the Dalai Lama was being welcomed in Washington.

China's heavy-handed response to the first incident had backfired. Just four days later on October 1, the founding anniversary of the People's Republic of China, another group of monks, this time from Sera Monastery, staged a demonstration to support the Dalai Lama and demand the release of the Drepung monks who had been arrested on September 27. Onlookers joined them, and the crowd of demonstrators swelled to around 3,000.[79] The monks were arrested immediately, then taken to a nearby police station and beaten. A crowd of Tibetans gathered outside the police station, demanding the release of the monks. Someone set fire to the police station, while others rushed in to rescue the prisoners. The police shot at the crowd, killing anywhere between 6 and 20 Tibetans.[80] The protests and the riots were brutally suppressed by the police, but not before news of China's crackdown reached the world through foreigners who smuggled photos of the demonstrations which were later disseminated in international

---

[76] Nonviolence International, *Truth is Our Only Weapon: The Tibetan Nonviolent Struggle*, (Bangkok, August 2000), 17.
[77] Ibid.
[78] Ibid, 14.
[79] Tibet Information Network, Reported Demonstrations 1987-96.
[80] Goldstein, *The Snow Lion and the Dragon*, 80.

media. These incidents bolstered the Dalai Lama's standing as Tibet's true representative, dealing a devastating blow to Beijing's image.

China's harsh suppression of dissent did not stem the tide of protests. The theme of these protests was decidedly political rather than religious — they overwhelmingly called for Tibetan independence. From September to December 1987, Lhasa witnessed eight protest incidents. In 1988, there were more than 17 demonstrations, of which 14 were pro-independence. The largest one, with around 2,000 people, took place on March 5, ending in riots and five deaths. In 1989, the year the Dalai Lama was awarded the Nobel Peace Prize, there were 34 protest incidents, of which 18 were pro-independence. The year ended in the implementation of martial law, but the demonstrations continued. In 1990, 12 of 18 major gatherings were pro-independence; in 1991, 26 of 30 incidents called for independence; in 1992, 20 of 22 demanded independence; and in 1993, there were 49 protest incidents, 31 of which were pro-independence.[81]

Notwithstanding the prominence of the street demonstrations, protest was not the only tactic used by Tibetans during this period. What follows is the examination of nonviolent tactics that Tibetans used from 1987 to 1993, when their activism was at its height.

Analyzing the Strategy and Tactics of the Uprising

Unlike the first Tibetan uprising of 1956-59, the second uprising was largely a nonviolent affair with a few episodes of limited violence. Over the course of six years, the demonstrations spiraled into riots only three times, in 1987, 1988 and 1989. The Tibetans strategically targeted a global audience with their message, and their protests were aimed at giving the Dalai Lama all the legitimacy he needed to represent them to foreign governments. Therefore, their priority was to maintain nonviolent discipline in keeping with the Dalai Lama's emphasis on peace. Tactically, they employed a range of nonviolent methods: demonstrations, marches, circumambulation, displaying the Tibetan national flag, chanting slogans and so forth.

---

[81] Tibet Information Network, Reported Demonstrations 1987-96.

Street Demonstration

The most visible form of protest in this uprising was the street demonstration. Both Tibetan activists and Chinese authorities saw this tactic as the ultimate challenge to Chinese rule. The street demonstration served multiple purposes: it expressed Tibetan opposition to Chinese rule, exposed China's brutalities to the world, and provided momentum to the resistance. While the street demonstration was the most visible, photographable and newsworthy tactic, it was highly risky and costly. Taking part in a demonstration almost guaranteed one's arrest, imprisonment and torture.

The demonstrations of 1987, writes Ronald Schwartz, produced a "pattern of performance that became the model of protest in Lhasa over the next six years. Thus protest became ritualized, assuming the same symbolic form every time it occurred." He ascribes two motives to the act of protest. First, through protest Tibetans were able to "overcome their objective powerlessness, and experience both solidarity and equality as they mutually acknowledge their common nationhood." Second, Tibetans were using the ritual of protest as a "substitute for licensed political discourse and communication."[82]

However, while the street demonstration became the most popular tactic, its deployment suffered from a lack of planning, discipline and coordination. Almost every major demonstration was driven by a strong element of spontaneity, which raised the level of unpredictability. On October 6, 1987, when a group of 50 young monks from the Drepung monastery were on their way to Lhasa to protest the government's continued detention of the 21 monks who had staged the September 27 demonstration, a Western witness asked the monks what they were planning to do when they arrived at the government building. They "answered that they didn't know."[83] After assembling in front of the government building, they started chanting slogans. A few minutes later they were arrested and "viciously beaten with belts, sticks, rifles, and pieces of metal."[84]

This seemingly mundane exchange between the monks and the Western witness reveals a deeper weakness of the Tibetan resistance: the lack of planning endemic to these street demonstrations. Every demonstration during this uprising was started by a small

---

[82] Schwartz, *Circle of Protest*, 20.
[83] Ibid.
[84] Ibid.

group of monks or nuns who rarely spent more than a few days planning their actions, and they subsequently spent years in prison. Many of the demonstrations that started with roughly a dozen monks or nuns ballooned into marches involving hundreds of people, all of whom joined on the spot, without prior planning or organizing. The protesters displayed incredible courage: they endured beatings, torture and imprisonment. But courage alone could not compensate for a lack of strategy.

The spontaneous nature of the demonstrations in 1987, 1988 and 1989 allowed them to easily spiral out of control and turn violent, making the demonstrators harder to control and more vulnerable to police brutality. Each time a protest turned into a riot, it was the spontaneous participation of lay people that tipped the balance toward violence. Perhaps the high degree of mental and behavioral training involved in monastic life made the monks and nuns, on the other hand, naturally more disciplined than others. Moreover, the monastics had been part of the actions from the planning stage, while lay Tibetans joined the demonstrations later, which made them more volatile than the monastics. The breakdown of nonviolent discipline was promptly and shrewdly used as a tool by the Chinese communist government in its propaganda. The Chinese government broadcast video footage of Tibetans engaged in property destruction to defame the Tibetan struggle, undermine international solidarity for Tibet, and mobilize Chinese public opinion against Tibetan aspirations for freedom.

Almost every major demonstration was driven by a strong element of spontaneity, which raised the level of unpredictability.

The lack of planning can partly be explained by the absence of space for organizing. China closely monitored communication among Tibetans by using tactics such as planting informants and tapping phone lines. Recruiting participants to join an action weeks in advance increased the chances of their being apprehended. Thus, the level of secrecy demanded by the political environment made planning extremely difficult. At the same time, activists were not experienced with this type of underground work. Therefore, for the monks and nuns, protest often became an end in and of itself rather than a means to achieve a specific end – a symbolic act rather than an instrumental or strategic one. They were, for example, not seeking a means of protest that would allow them to avoid arrest. In fact, their sole intention was to go to prison. In some contexts, this type of action can overwhelm police and generate greater publicity for a campaign.

However, this would require greater tactical diversity involving alternation between acts of omission to commission to maintain momentum than was present in the Tibetan case. Their strategic logic was that they would suffer in prison so that their suffering could be used as political capital by those outside, specifically the global Free Tibet movement, to delegitimize Chinese rule.

Poster Campaigns

Protesters also employed other tactics that were slightly less risky. The creation of poster campaigns was a highly popular tactic. Poster campaigns were an ideal covert tactic in Lhasa, deployed among the city's labyrinthine alleys late at night. Tibetan activists sneaked out at night and put up posters in Tibetan, Chinese and English, calling for the "independence of Tibet," for the Chinese to "quit Tibet," and for the long life of the Dalai Lama. Poster campaigns served many purposes: they "communicate[d] to the Chinese and the world Tibet's desire for independence; encourage[d] the Tibetan population to unite in the struggle for independence; and serve[d] to educate Tibetans on such issues as human rights and Tibet's political status."[85]

Through poster campaigns, Tibetans were also able to introduce an element of subversive humor into their activism. In 1991, at the height of the poster campaign's popularity, Chinese authorities were dispatching squads of policemen at night to stop poster-pasting activities. One night, as the poster removal squad returned to their headquarters after their nightly round, they found the entire police station "completely covered with pro-independence leaflets."[86] Stories of humor such as this turn ordinary political incidents into memorable anecdotes that expose the weakness of the regime, making it a subject of ridicule rather than fear.

Sometimes, the walls became a platform for debate and rebuttal, as Tibetan activists used posters not only as a proactive tool to educate people but also as a reactive tool to challenge the government's announcements. In 1993, when the Chinese government, in an attempt to discourage separatism, warned that all Tibetans holding official positions in the Tibetan Autonomous Region government would lose their jobs

---

[85] Nonviolence International, *Truth is Our Only Weapon*, 15.
[86] Ibid., 17.

if Tibet became independent, the Tibetan activists immediately responded with posters citing the Dalai Lama's promise that in the event of a free Tibet, Tibetan officials in Tibet would retain their positions while the exile government would be dissolved.[87]

Distribution of Literature

Another immensely popular tactic was the production and distribution of contraband literature: pamphlets, leaflets and books about human rights, democracy and Tibetan history. This literature was distributed with the goal of raising political awareness. Some of the most popular items that circulated in Tibet in the 1980s and early 90s were Tibetan translations of the Universal Declaration of Human Rights, the Dalai Lama's autobiography and the Five-Point Peace Plan.[88] According to a former monk from the Ganden monastery, they would "print literature in the forms of letters, brochures, and pamphlets and keep them in places of high foot traffic, such as the Barkor Lingkor, as well as tying them with prayer flags." Since they do not require face-to-face contact, these creative methods of disseminating literature lowered the activists' risk of being identified by the police. Leaflets and pamphlets placed anonymously at holy sites would safely find their way into the hands of Tibetans without being intercepted by Chinese police.

Graffiti

Graffiti was used occasionally during this period. In July 1992, a monk named Lobsang and his friends painted independence slogans on the wall of a local bank and along the main street in Chideshol, Lhokha Prefecture.[89] Tibetans painted protest graffiti on various surfaces, including the walls of government buildings, monasteries and bumpers of vehicles belonging to township officials.[90]

---

[87] Robert Barnett, *The Development of Nonviolent Protest in Tibet* (August 6, 1991).
[88] Nonviolence International, *Truth is Our Only Weapon*, 17. The Five-Point Peace Plan refers to the proposal made by the Dalai Lama to the Chinese government in 1988, which suggested turning Tibet into a demilitarized zone of peace.
[89] Human Rights Update, Tibetan Center for Human Rights and Democracy (May 31, 1997).
[90] Nonviolence International, *Truth is Our Only Weapon*, 16.

Kora – Circumambulation[91]

Ordinary Tibetans' worldview, fundamentally shaped by Buddhism, played a central role in determining their choice of tactics. In 1987, almost every demonstration began with the ritual of circumambulating the Jokhang, an act of profound religious symbolism. By circling the Jokhang, the monks incorporated the kora or circumambulation, a common manifestation of faith, into the spectrum of political resistance.[92] A daily routine was transformed into an act of resistance, lowering the threshold for participation in the resistance. In the following months, Tibetans poured into the Barkor Square to offer prayers, circle the Jokhang, burn incense and fly prayer flags. Even if the Chinese authorities knew that these religious acts concealed a political motivation, there was no way for them to prove and punish them short of totalitarian-like retribution.

Protest Singing

Singing as a protest tactic became wildly popular in Tibet during the 1990s, especially among political prisoners. One of the most famous cases of protest singing involved 14 nuns in Drapchi prison who secretly recorded freedom songs. Once the tapes were smuggled into India, their songs were reproduced and distributed through hundreds of cassette tapes. The nuns became known as the Drapchi 14. Their forbidden music was used by rights organizations to publicize the nuns' plight and build international pressure for their release. "Protest singing is found across Tibet at grassroots level, in prisons, and more surprisingly, in commercial entertainment venues and on pop music albums; it may be private, discrete or confrontational," writes Tibetan music and dance scholar Anna Morcom.[93]

---

[91] See footnote #71 in Chapter 5 for a complete definition of this term.
[92] Nonviolence International, *Truth is Our Only Weapon*, 17.
[93] Anna Morcom, *Unity and Discord*.

Chapter 5: The Second Tibetan Uprising (1987-89)

Noncooperation

Compared with the variety of protest methods used during this period, Tibetans barely explored the noncooperation or nonviolent intervention methods.[94] In 1988 and 1989, the monks in Lhasa boycotted the annual state-sanctioned Monlam Prayer Festival to embarrass the government officials, who wanted high attendance at the festival to impress outsiders.[95] Due to the monks' boycott, the festival was canceled, denying the Chinese authorities the opportunity to use the festival as a propaganda tool. However, in general, the use of noncooperation was consistently limited throughout this period. Why did noncooperation tactics remain largely unexplored, particularly in an environment where protest tactics were highly dangerous and costly?

A daily routine was transformed into an act of resistance, lowering the threshold for participation in the resistance.

One factor was the Tibetans' lack of access to information about other nonviolent struggles – no doubt the result of China's censorship and the dearth of Tibetan language literature on nonviolent resistance. While many Tibetans were familiar with iconic personalities like Mahatma Gandhi, Martin Luther King, Jr. and Nelson Mandela, they were far from being well versed in the details of the nonviolent campaigns these figured planned and led.[96] This lack of knowledge about stories of nonviolent resistance naturally reduced the spectrum of options available, or imaginable.

Traditionally among Tibetans, bravery and courage commanded more respect than strategy and cunning. The tendency to glorify valor as a highly prized virtue is not unique to Tibetans, who have a deeply mythologized warrior culture. Another relevant example can be Poland, where valor is glorified by historians, poets, filmmakers and politicians. "Valor is attached to knightly or soldierly virtues and unquestioned martyrdom for the Polish fatherland and the country's freedom," writes Maciej Bartkowski in one of

---

[94] The definitions of these methods can be found in Figure 5 in Chapter 9.
[95] Schwartz, *Circle of Protest*.
[96] One of the Tibetans who arrived in India from Tibet recently told the author that in the 1980s, Tibetans knew very little even about the Indian freedom struggle other than the fact that it was led by Gandhi. They knew almost nothing about the details of the Indian noncooperation and civil disobedience campaigns that crippled British rule.

several chapters that highlight similar cases of glorification in other countries in the edited volume *Recovering Nonviolent History*.[97] This visceral inclination for applauding valor is another reason Tibetans have used protest tactics more frequently than noncooperation. The former is dramatic and high-risk while the latter is often invisible and low-risk. The low-key nature of noncooperation tactics rendered them unattractive to those who believed that an opponent as big as China could be effectively challenged only with tactics that were equally epic and dramatic.

---

[97] Bartkowski, *Recovering Nonviolent History*, 260.

Chapter 6
The Rise and Fall of Global Grassroots Mobilization (1989-2002)

Dharamsala's new strategy of "internationalization," accompanied by the protests in Lhasa, produced two important results that transformed the Tibetan struggle: the support of Western governments and the rise in international grassroots activism for Tibet.

Legislative Support in the West

The high-profile protests in Lhasa propelled the Tibetan independence movement into primetime news, turning it into a defining political cause of the decade. When the Nobel Peace Prize was awarded to the Dalai Lama in 1989, it crystallized the nobility of the Tibetan cause in Western public consciousness. The issue gathered seemingly unstoppable momentum. It was during this period that the Tibetan leadership began to make serious inroads into legislatures around the world, most prominently in US Congress. Leading senators and congressmen from the Democratic as well as the Republican parties became enduring champions of Tibet, turning the issue into one of the few bipartisan causes in both chambers of Congress. Resolutions were passed in Congress as well as other parliaments recognizing the Dalai Lama as the legitimate leader of the Tibetan people and condemning China's occupation of Tibet.[98]

A European Parliament resolution was passed on October 14, 1987, "recalling that both during the early days of the Chinese occupation in the 1950s and during the Cultural Revolution the Tibetan religion and culture were brutally repressed." US Congress passed a stronger resolution on December 22, 1987, stating that the "Chinese Communist army

---
[98] Tom Grunfeld, *The Making of Modern Tibet* (New York: M.E. Sharpe, 1996), 232.

invaded and occupied Tibet." And it went further: "Over 1,000,000 Tibetans perished from 1959 to 1979 as a direct result of the political instability, executions, imprisonment and large-scale famine engendered by the policies of the People's Republic of China in Tibet."[99] From 1987 to 1997, Congress passed some 20 resolutions on Tibet, and the European Parliament passed at least 12.[100]

Although these resolutions did not have the coercive power to bring China to the table to negotiate the future of Tibet, they inflicted a significant political and moral cost on the Chinese government. For one, the resolutions were seen as a political verdict in the court of global public opinion; each resolution chipped away at China's reputation. More importantly, some of these resolutions brought concrete gains to the Tibetan independence movement. For example, one of Dharamsala's greatest challenges was communicating with its constituency in Tibet. But this challenge was partly resolved in 1991 when, thanks to an Act of Congress, Voice of America (VOA) created a Tibetan service and launched a program that broadcast to listeners inside Tibet.[101]

However, as China's value as a trading partner rose in the early 1990s, economics began to overshadow rights-based politics. The Cold War-era containment policy was replaced by a policy of engagement with China. While legislative bodies churned out strongly worded resolutions supporting Tibet, the governments of these countries rushed to sign trade deals with China. As the gap between the legislative and executive branches of governments grew more pronounced, Dharamsala recognized the strategic inadequacy of using Western legislatures as leverage to pressure China.

Global Grassroots Mobilization and the Rise of Pro-Tibet NGOs

Perhaps the most significant outcome of Dharamsala's strategic recalibration and the protests in Lhasa was the rise of international grassroots mobilization for Tibet. The

---

[99] Tibet Justice Center, Legal Materials on Tibet. This center is an NGO based in California, which conducted research to build a legal and historical case for Tibetan self-determination.
[100] Ibid. and Department of Information and International Relations, International Resolutions and Recognitions on Tibet: 1959-1997.
[101] Shakya, *The Dragon in the Land of Snows*, 434. Soon after the establishment of the VOA Tibetan service, Radio Free Asia also launched a Tibetan service and started broadcasting daily to listeners in Tibet.

Chapter 6: The Rise and Fall of Global Grassroots Mobilization (1989-2002)

Dalai Lama's trips to the West set off a chain of events, the most seminal of which was a series of Tibetan Freedom Concerts, organized by Adam Yauch of the Beastie Boys, held in New York City, San Francisco and Washington, DC.[102] The concerts, attended by hundreds of thousands, became a landmark cultural event in the United States; Tibet went from being an obscure issue into a cause célèbre overnight.

To harness the rise of public and youth interest in the issue, dozens of organizations were established, including the aforementioned Students for a Free Tibet, the International Campaign for Tibet, and the Free Tibet Campaign. More groups continued to emerge in dozens of countries, mobilizing thousands of volunteers in activities ranging from rallies to petition drives to direct actions. The various advocacy groups represented a new kind of political capital for Dharamsala. This global grassroots force, led by NGOs which were propelled by people power rather than legislative support, was unencumbered by the political parameters of congressional politics. Furthermore, the fulcrum at which this new power was directed was not the Congress or the White House but the business sector.

The leading NGOs in the Tibet movement waged a series of nonviolent campaigns targeting multinational institutions seeking to invest in China. The most famous of these campaigns was waged in 1999, when the World Bank was on the verge of granting a $160 million loan to China to move 58,000 Chinese farmers into Tibet. As the bank's largest borrower, it seemed a forgone conclusion that China would receive the loan. However, pro-Tibetan independence activists – a coalition including the International Campaign for Tibet and Students for a Free Tibet – organized several months of protest rallies outside the bank, prompting it to commission an independent review of the project. The review found that the bank's staff had violated 7 of 10 operational directives.[103] The campaigners mobilized their grassroots members to send around "500 emails a day to all 24 of (the bank's) executive directors during the weeks leading up to the vote," which resulted in the bank needing a "fax line dedicated for correspondence on the Tibet-China project alone."[104]

At a Tibetan Freedom Concert in Chicago during this period, Students for a

---

[102] Los Angeles Times Blog, Tibet activist Erin Potts' pays tribute to Adam Yauch, 8 May 2012. Also see A History of the Milarepa Fund at www.beastiemania.com.
[103] Probe International Journal, World Bank cancels China Tibet resettlement scheme, November 1999.
[104] Nonviolence International, *Truth is Our Only Weapon*, 41.

Free Tibet "collected 17,000 signatures on petitions and sent 6,000 emails and faxes" addressed to the bank, expressing opposition to the project.[105] Two activists from Students for a Free Tibet scaled the bank's façade and hung a banner that read: "World Bank Approves China's Genocide in Tibet." This dramatic action made the headlines on all major international news outlets, causing unprecedented damage to the World Bank's reputation. A senior officer of the bank said, "I have not seen anything have this profound an effect on this institution in the seven years I've worked at the Bank. I think it has changed the way people inside the Bank think. The Tibet groups have waged the most intelligent and measured campaign the Bank has ever seen."[106] Finally, as a result of several months of protest and negative publicity in the media, the loan was canceled. This high-profile political defeat caused enormous humiliation to China in the global arena.[107]

This campaign stands out as a great example of strategic planning; the campaigners chose the perfect combination of targets, timing and tactics. This was the first time that the movement was able to deal a concrete, measurable blow to China's interest by using nonviolent means. Journalist Sebastian Mallaby, who wrote an article in *Foreign Policy* scorning the Tibet movement and defending the World Bank, remarked with disbelief: "The Lilliputian activists had taken on the bank, and they had won the first round."[108]

The Tibet movement was galvanized by this unprecedented victory. In the years that followed, this coalition of Tibet groups, often working in tandem with Dharamsala, battled corporations contemplating investment in China's exploitative projects in Tibet. In 2003, the Australia Tibet Council stopped Sino Gold from mining in Tibet.[109] Some say the mining giant Rio Tinto's decision not to dig in Tibet a few years later was based on a fear of the political minefield that Tibet had become. The Tibet movement's grassroots muscle and its ability to generate negative publicity, posed a real threat to these companies' brand names and affected their decision-making.[110]

---

[105] Ibid.

[106] Ibid.

[107] *Pittsburgh Post-Gazette*, World Bank rejects controversial loan to China, 8 July 2000.

[108] Sebastian Mallaby, "NGOs: Fighting Poverty, Hurting the Poor," *Foreign Policy Magazine*, September/October 2004.

[109] *Sydney Morning Herald*, "Sino Gold digs itself a hole in Tibet," 13 May 2003, http://www.smh.com.au/articles/2003/05/16/1052885400212.html

[110] In a 2013 article in *The Street*, "Foreign Business in Tibet? Investors Beware," Ralph Jennings writes, "Whether or not Tibet has gained from China's investment since the railway opened in 2006, activist groups have come down hard on participating international companies, usually those in mining or tourism. Their well-practiced global publicity campaigns have dented the reputations of firms in Tibet and discouraged other companies from making the long railway journey at all."

Chapter 6: The Rise and Fall of Global Grassroots Mobilization (1989-2002)

The reach of this grassroots movement further multiplied when thousands of Tibetans immigrated to the West in the 1990s. The new Tibetan communities in the West, while working with advocacy groups, organized demonstrations against visiting Chinese leaders. It became impossible for high-profile Chinese leaders to visit Western capitals without being hounded by hundreds of pro-Tibet protesters. The woes that the protests caused the Chinese leaders were revealed in the leaked transcript of a speech by Zhao Qizheng, Minister of the Information Office of the State Council, at a conference in 2000: "During every foreign visit of our leaders last year, the Dalai clique, with covert incitement and help from Western countries as well as Tibet Support Groups, interfered and created disruption through protest rallies. In this way, they gained the highest-level international platform and intervention."[111]

Start of Dialogue, End of Mobilization

This golden era of global grassroots advocacy for Tibet ended in 2002, when Beijing invited the Dalai Lama's envoys to a round of talks. A few months before, Beijing had won the bid to host the 2008 Olympics, and many Tibetans suspected that Beijing's only motivation was to mute international criticism of its Tibet policy ahead of the Olympic Games. Their suspicions would later be affirmed by the revelations of a high-level Chinese diplomat, Chen Yonglin, who defected from the Chinese embassy in Australia in 2005. Responding to a question about the Sino-Tibetan dialogue, he said that it was merely a tactic and that there was "no sincerity from the Chinese side."[112] But Dharamsala took the bait and entered the dialogue without setting any preconditions. For China, merely holding the dialogue constituted victory: simply by talking to the Dalai Lama's envoys, China was able to muzzle international criticism of its record in Tibet. Beijing's subtext was: since the Chinese and the Tibetans were talking directly with each other, third parties should no longer interfere in the issue.

One of Beijing's demands during the initial rounds of dialogue, unsurprisingly, was that Dharamsala tone down the international protests against China.[113] Anxious not to

---

[111] See the leaked transcript of a speech delivered in 2000 by Zhao Qizheng, Minister of Information Office of China's State Council: https://studentsforafreetibet.org/get-involved/action-toolbox/tibet-related-external-propaganda-and-tibetology-work-in-the-new-era.
[112] Warren Smith, *China's Tibet? Autonomy or Assimilation* (Lanham: Rowman and Littlefield Publishers, 2008), 257.
[113] Ibid, 228.

derail the dialogue, Dharamsala decided to invest in trust building, and began promoting a policy of "creating a conducive environment" for the talks. The Tibetan government issued a series of appeals from 2002 to 2006, urging the global Tibet movement to hold off on their protests and agitating actions.[114] The Tibetan Prime Minister Samdhong Rinpoche saw dialogue and protest as mutually exclusive. Now that dialogue had been started, he reasoned, protest would be unnecessary. In reality, his appeal prematurely forfeited a tactic that had proven effective at making China see the value of dialogue in the first place.

> *The Tibetan side, not recognizing Beijing's vulnerability at the time, did not set preconditions for entering the dialogue and ensuring its authentic nature.*

This period witnessed a growing disconnect between Dharamsala and the global grassroots movement. Many Tibetans and activists in the independence movement saw Dharamsala's appeals to suspend protests as an appeasement for China. On the other hand, Dharamsala came to view the independence movement as a liability and, even worse, an obstruction to the progress of dialogue with Beijing.[115]

In hindsight, Dharamsala's bargaining power in the years leading up to the Beijing Olympics was perhaps the highest it had ever been. To fulfill its aim of hosting a protest-free Olympics, China may have been more willing than usual to make certain concessions such as granting mass amnesty to Tibetan political prisoners. The Tibetan side, not recognizing Beijing's vulnerability at the time, did not set preconditions for entering the dialogue and ensuring its authentic nature. Beijing had already obtained what it wanted from the moment the Tibetans sat down for the first round of talks. China's strategy for

---

[114] Prime Minister Samdhong Rinpoche issued subsequent appeals to Tibet support groups in October 2002, September 2005, and April 2006 urging them to refrain from protests during Chinese leaders' trips to the West.

[115] Samdhong Rinpoche said in an appeal to the Tibet groups in April 2006: "President Hu Jintao will soon pay an official visit to America this month and the Kashag would like to once again strongly appeal with utmost importance and emphasis to all the Tibetans and Tibet Support Groups to refrain from any activities, including staging of protest demonstrations causing embarrassment to him. This appeal is not only to create a conducive atmosphere for negotiations but also not to cause embarrassment and difficulty to His Holiness the Dalai Lama whose visit coincides with President Hu Jintao's visit to America. If protests are held, this will give the impression that no Tibetan or Tibet Support Group is taking notice of and carrying out His Holiness the Dalai Lama's instructions issued in the recent March 10th statement. Therefore, to avoid such things from happening, the Kashag hopes and believes that, unlike last year, all Tibetans and Tibet support groups will respond positively to this appeal at least for this one time, and make a wise choice from a wider perspective." To access the full appeal, see the Central Tibetan Administration's website: http://tibet.net/about-tibet/worldwide-tibet-movement/.

Chapter 6: The Rise and Fall of Global Grassroots Mobilization (1989-2002)

the dialogue, writes Warren Smith, "seemed to be to appear conciliatory while making no actual concessions."[116] By the time the dialogue between the two sides stalled in 2008, and eventually collapsed in 2010 after nine rounds of talks, Dharamsala had little to show for it. Instead, it was left with diminished momentum for an international grassroots movement, having lost the mission-oriented clarity of earlier years. As for Tibetans themselves, many became convinced that the process was simply Beijing's ploy to temper international criticism of its Tibet policy ahead of the Olympics.

---

[116] Smith, China's Tibet?, 232.

Chapter 7
The Third Uprising (2008)

While the exiled grassroots movement reached its peak in the 1990s, the resistance inside Tibet hit an impasse. China's Tibet policy, which combined political restrictions with a stream of economic subsidies, had managed to root out dissent and crush all signs of organized resistance. On the international stage, China's astronomical economic growth captivated the West, and governments started warming up to Beijing. At the turn of the millennium, except for the occasional protest by a lone monk or nun, the restive Himalayan nation seemed subdued.

Therefore, it took the world by surprise when Tibet erupted in a nationwide uprising in 2008 that surpassed the earlier two popular revolts in breadth, scope and duration. Unlike the previous two uprisings, this one spread to all three historical provinces of Tibet (see Figure 3 in Chapter 3) within days, and it endured in other forms of resistance despite China's crackdown. How did it happen? What were the conditions and factors that led to this unprecedented event? What was the nature of the resistance during this period?

Cultural Preparation for Political Mobilization

Although the uprising caught both Beijing and Dharamsala off guard, it did not come out of thin air. From 2001 to 2007, many aspects of Tibetan culture – language, music, art and literature – witnessed a revival similar to the one that occurred in the 1980s. This cultural renaissance created a sense of Tibetan pride, reinforcing a pan-Tibetan identity across the plateau.

This time, the renaissance came from the periphery and spread to the center, originating in eastern Tibet, where China's policies had been less draconian than in the Tibetan Autonomous Region. Partly because of the incorporation of eastern Tibet into the Chinese provinces of Sichuan, Qinghai, Gansu and Yunan, and partly because Beijing saw the TAR as the more politicized region and thus potentially more rebellious to its rule, Tibetans in the TAR were denied certain freedoms enjoyed by those in eastern Tibet. For example, the Dalai Lama's photograph, which was strictly banned in the TAR, was ubiquitous in eastern Tibet. In Kham and Amdo, Tibetans often discussed sociopolitical issues that would be considered off limits in Lhasa, where the "walls had ears," meaning informants were everywhere.

From 2001 to 2007, eastern Tibet became the crossroads where several socioeconomic factors intersected: growth in Tibetan spending power, the rise of the musician as a social leader and public opinion maker, and the proliferation of communication tools and technologies. First, Tibetan spending power rose dramatically during this period. According to Chinese government statistics, the Tibetan per capita GDP was RMB[117] 702 in 1984, RMB 5,324 in 2001, and RMB 13,861 in 2008.[118] The sharp economic growth was driven partly by the rise in the trade of caterpillar fungus, a medicinal Tibetan herb that was in high demand in the Chinese aphrodisiac industry.[119] For many families, picking caterpillar fungus during the summer months became an easy way to generate income.[120]

As Tibetans began earning more, they started investing in arts and cultural entertainment by organizing events that celebrated Tibetan culture. Held in the rolling grasslands of Amdo and Kham, events such as the annual concerts in Rebkong or the horse racing festivals in Lithang drew crowds that numbered in the thousands. These festivals brought the most popular musicians from across Tibet – Yadong and Kunga from Kham, Sherten and Jamyang Kyi from Amdo, and so on. They sang about Tibetan pride, unity and destiny. The new music by singers from eastern Tibet, whose bold lyrics carried references to the Dalai Lama and Tibetan political aspirations, became wildly popular.

One of the most widely shared Tibetan music videos during this period was

---

[117] RMB is short for Renminbi, the Chinese currency.
[118] Tibet Online, Report on the Economic and Social Development of Tibet, 31 March 2009, http://en.people.cn/90001/90776/90785/6625577.html.
[119] Barbara Demick, *Los Angeles Times*, "In Tibet, A Worm Worth Its Weight in Gold," 27 June 2008, http://www.latimes.com/world/asia/la-fg-worm27-2008jun27-story.html#page=1.
[120] The harvest of caterpillar fungus, a medicinal herb that sells for astronomical prices in China, has produced an economic boom in Tibet for the moment. Some raise concerns that this trade, which preoccupies Tibetans of every age for several months during the picking season and keeps children out of school, is undermining the long-term development of human and social capital.

Kunga's "Hope and Sorrow," a 2006 song that expresses sorrow over not having the opportunity to meet the "three brothers," presumably the Dalai Lama, the Panchen Lama and the Karmapa. This video, which used an image of the sun to represent the Dalai Lama, became a YouTube sensation in Tibetan cyberspace. Another singer, Drolma Kyab, performed a song called "Mentally Return" on live television, skillfully using metaphorical descriptions that referred to "Tibet and Tibetans to create a bridge between Tibetans inside and outside of China."[121] The live performance of this song, in the words of Cameron Warner, can be seen as an open invitation to exiled Tibetans to imagine their return to Tibet.

The snow-capped mountains are heavenly fences
In the blue rivers float the ornaments of the sun and moon
The vast green pastures are the stars' beds
This holy land, which was formed through a hole in the sky,
"The Roof of the World," the rich Land of Snows,
It is our fatherland, Tibetans of the Snow Land!
The six reincarnating beings are our kind parents
Peace and non-violence are our thoughts,
Bravery is our fortitude
The people who abide in the land of the Snow Mountains,
The first to hold this high plateau,
It's us the red-faced Tibetans of the Snow Land!
Oh Brothers and Sisters! Tibetans!
We came here remembering your profound love and friendship,
Today, in front of you we perform a dance!
Oh Brothers and Sisters! Tibetans!
This is a dance taught by you,
This is a gift to celebrate meeting our brothers and sisters!

This song was first performed publicly in July 2006 at the Rebkong concert,

---

[121] Cameron Warner, "Hope and Sorrow: Uncivil Religion, Tibetan Music Videos and YouTube," in *Ethnos: Journal of Anthropology*, 11 January 2013, 8.

giving way later to a march of 100 Tibetan exiles from Dharamsala to Tibet.[122] Organized by the six leading Tibetan NGOs in India, this march was announced in January 2008 and launched two months later, sending waves of excitement throughout the community. Broadcast over Radio Free Asia, Voice of Tibet and VOA, the monks in the great monasteries of Lhasa were enthralled by the news of the march.[123] Though Indian police eventually stopped the participants at the Indo-Tibet border three months after the march began, it had already begun to energize the uprising.

Although musical gatherings on the same scale as those in Kham and Amdo were not allowed in central Tibet, CDs and DVDs of these concerts lined the streets of Lhasa, as vendors blasted their music in Barkor Square. Through the Internet, these music videos made their way into exile and to the top of the Tibetan diaspora playlist. At the same time, the music of Tibetan singers in exile also found its way into Tibet. Vendors in Lhasa sold pirated CDs of exiled pop stars like Phurbu T. Namgyal and Tsering Gyurme.[124] Music became a lifeline for Tibetans, delivering messages of hope and longing back and forth across the Himalayas, strengthening the bond between Tibetans in Tibet and those in exile. This spawned an era of musical interactions between the different regions, while deepening a sense of national political consciousness. As the power of music helped Tibetans overcome regional or sectarian divides, it became a vehicle for unity and a means of mobilization.

Perhaps one of the most interesting yet overlooked factors behind the political reawakening of Tibetans was the release in 2007 of Windows Vista, which carried a built-in Tibetan font and keyboard in Unicode standard.[125] Until about 2005, using Tibetan on a computer was a maddening process that required the user to download and install font and keyboard software. Depending on the font the user chose, s/he could not read any content written in other fonts although that content was composed in the Tibetan language. This created a digital barrier between Tibetans in exile and

---

[122] Heather Timmons, "Tibetan Protest Marchers Vow to Reach Homeland," *The New York Times*, 12 March 2008.

[123] A Tibetan pilgrim from Lhasa whom the author interviewed in February 2008 in Dharamsala said that news of the exiles' planned march to Tibet had captivated the monks of the three great monasteries in Lhasa, with some of the Lhasa Tibetans suggesting that they should travel to the Indian border to receive their brethren.

[124] Tibetans, like many other people in the developing world, have a generous attitude toward piracy of intangible products like music.

[125] The Tibetan and Himalayan Library, A New Chapter in Tibetan Computing, http://www.thlib.org/tools/scripts/wiki/a%20new%20chapter%20in%20tibetan%20computing.html.

Chapter 7: The Third Uprising (2008)

their brethren in Tibet. However, after the invention of the Tibetan Unicode font and its release on Microsoft tools, and later on Apple's iPhones, Tibetans in Tibet could read email messages and Internet content that came from Tibetans in exile without needing to download any additional software, and vice versa.[126]

This game-changing innovation revolutionized trans-Himalayan communication, facilitating unprecedented exchange and discussion among Tibetans.[127] Tibetans in Tibet routinely communicated with exiles, breaking through the Great Firewall with circumvention technologies – sending text messages, making Skype calls, and chatting over QQ, the Chinese version of Skype. The geographical divide between Dharamsala and its constituency in Tibet suddenly became irrelevant.

As the scope of commerce and communication increased, so did Tibetan grievances against China, the most serious of which were directed towards the new "sky railway." In 2006, China completed the construction of the Beijing-Lhasa railway, which Tibetans shunned as a demographic death sentence. The railway brought a flood of Chinese settlers, making it harder for Tibetans to access employment, university admissions, and other opportunities. According to a US State Department report, "Among the approximately 2.35 million persons arriving in Lhasa from July 2006 to December 2007, more than a half million may have been non-Tibetan, mostly ethnic Han, workers, traders, and business persons who intended to remain for a period in the TAR to work, engage in business, or seek other economic opportunity[.]"[128]

Many foreigners and exiled Tibetans who traveled to Tibet in 2007 observed that the Beijing-Lhasa railway was the greatest source of Tibetan resentment against China. The unprecedented influx of Chinese settlers facilitated by the railway accentuated the distinction between Chinese and Tibetan culture, which made the Tibetans more determined to protect their culture from what they perceived as an existential threat to its survival. What Tibetans could not predict at the time was that this period of cultural revival and development of cultural capital would later become the foundation for a more robust resistance. In a way, culture was to become not only the end but also the

---

[126] "Otani Unicode Tibetan Language Kit now on MacOS X Leopard," Kyoto, Japan, 26 October 2007.
[127] Warner, "Hope and Sorrow," 15.
[128] Congressional-Executive Commission on China, Qinghai-Tibet Railway Statistics Add to Confusion, Mask Impact on Local Population, 4 March 2010.

means of the Tibetan resistance — in other words, transformative resistance.

2008: Nationwide Protests, Lhasa Riots

In March 2008, Tibet erupted in the largest uprising since 1959. Monks from the Drepung and Sera monasteries staged protest marches, raising the Tibetan national flag and shouting slogans "Freedom for Tibet," "Allow the return of the Dalai Lama," and "Independence for Tibet." Authorities arrested the monks and shut down the monasteries. More protests occurred in the next three days; they too were met with beatings and arrests.

On March 14, riots broke out in Lhasa. Lay Tibetans, who had been outraged by the sight of Chinese police beating the monks, attacked the security forces with rocks. When the security forces retreated, the emboldened protesters directed their wrath not only at symbols of Chinese rule, such as government buildings and police vehicles, but also at symbols of Chinese presence, such as Chinese-owned shops and businesses. These acts led to greater ethnic tension between the Tibetans and the Chinese.

According to Beijing, 18 civilians and one policeman died and 382 civilians were injured. According to Dharamsala and human rights groups, 220 Tibetans were killed, 5,600 arrested or detained, 1,294 injured, 290 sentenced and over 1,000 disappeared in the ensuing crackdown. From the start of the uprising in March until the Olympics in August, about 130 instances of protests had taken place in Tibet. Unlike the protests of the late 1980s, which were confined to central Tibet, the 2008 protests spanned all three historical provinces and engaged diverse demographics: monastics, students, teachers, traders, nomads, intellectuals and farmers. In fact, the vast majority of the protests occurred in Kham and Amdo, spreading to more than 52 counties across Tibet (see Figure 3 in Chapter 3).[129]

Nonviolent Discipline, Strategy and Unity

The uprising – especially the March 14 riots – was portrayed in the mainstream media as a sign of militant Tibetan youths discarding the Dalai Lama's nonviolent

---

[129] "A Great Mountain Burned by Fire," A Report by the International Campaign for Tibet, 22.

principles. The riots were broadcast repeatedly on Chinese and global television channels, an attempt to create the impression that the Tibetan struggle was turning violent. In reality, the 2008 uprising demonstrated a greater degree of nonviolent discipline than was the case during the previous two uprisings. The sensational headlines belied a more significant truth: the Tibetan struggle had been moving away from violence and toward a stronger commitment to nonviolent action over the course of half a century.

Statistically, there were at least 125 incidents of protest in 2008, the vast majority of which were peaceful. Only on March 14 in Lhasa and on March 28 in Machu were there incidents of violence in which Tibetans attacked Chinese civilians.[130] Limited violence on the part of the Tibetans was sufficiently visible that the Chinese propaganda machine used it to portray the Tibetan uprising as wholly violent and bloodthirsty. Time and again, any violent act by participants in a movement, no matter how limited and isolated, have benefited the oppressor far more than the oppressed.

The International Campaign for Tibet documented 15 other incidents of vandalism in which Tibetans caused damage to Chinese government property, like police stations or cars. Aside from these incidents, all other incidents of protest across Tibet were nonviolent. This was in fact a period when Tibetans demonstrated the highest commitment to nonviolent discipline to date.

China deployed its propaganda to paint protesters as violent to justify crackdowns on street demonstrations and the arrest of thousands of Tibetans. But the uprising proved resilient. Instead of dying out, the street demonstrations simply morphed into other kinds of resistance. This was the period when a new movement known as Lhakar was born.

The Lhakar Movement: Cultural Resistance

As China stamped out all forms of collective expressions of dissent, Tibetans responded by de-collectivizing their activism. The Lhakar movement (or the White Wednesday movement) emerged in late 2008 and has continued through today (2015), as Tibetans began taking part in small acts of resistance every Wednesday.[131]

---

[130] Ibid.
[131] Wednesday is the rla-sa (soul day) of the Dalai Lama, and Tibetans have a long tradition of conducting special rituals on this day to pray for their leader's health and longevity.

Through personal actions – wearing traditional clothes, eating Tibetan food, listening to independent radio, and using the Tibetan language at home – many Tibetans began to use their individual space to assert their collective identity, which had been suppressed for decades.

In this politically charged period, rituals that used to be purely cultural suddenly took on a political significance. Tibetans conducted these rituals in part to reinforce their national identity, but more so to assert a totally non-Chinese identity. In a zero-sum game of identity politics, being Tibetan became synonymous with "not being Chinese." This phenomenon gave rise to a series of practical actions that went beyond symbolism and, eventually, beyond a once-per-week affair. Turning their homes, workplaces and cyberspace into extended domains of resistance, Tibetans began to simultaneously open up more social, political and economic space. Emphasizing private acts of resistance over public acts of protest, Lhakar decentralized the resistance and empowered the individual. Rather than expecting freedom to come from a top-down policy in Beijing, people started to control their own daily thoughts, decisions and actions, thereby creating a parallel world of freedom alongside China's superstructure of repression and captivity.

> *For the first time in decades, perhaps centuries, Tibetans were wielding culture to save politics, instead of waiting for politics to save culture.*

In the past there was a notion, particularly among Tibetan elders, that a culture's survival was at the mercy of politics. However, the advent of Lhakar shattered this disempowering narrative. A growing number of Tibetans began using art, literature, poetry and music as vehicles for expressing their faith in the Dalai Lama, love of their homeland, and the desire for freedom. Songs with politically charged lyrics or music videos became hits.[132] For the first time in decades, perhaps centuries, Tibetans were wielding culture to save politics, instead of waiting for politics to save culture. Tibetans were finally tapping into their rich cultural heritage to produce a powerful set of nonviolent tools. In just a few years, the Lhakar movement has transformed Tibetan resistance.

---

[132] The Tibetan hip hop band Yudrug became a household name when their music gained overnight popularity both in Tibet and in exile after they released "New Generation," a defiant anthem of resistance set to an equally raucous rap beat.

Parallel Institution-Building

During this period, the focus of activism has shifted from purely agitating tactics of protest to more constructive, decentralized and widespread acts of noncooperation and parallel institution building. This process of creative resistance continues today. Studying the Tibetan language has become the most popular form of the constructive program: underground language schools have blossomed as monasteries and volunteer teachers began holding Tibetan language classes in the prayer halls. These underground classes are being attended by hundreds of children. In fact, some of these schools became so successful that the Chinese authorities have shut them down.[133]

In various parts of Tibet, people have taken pledges to speak pure Tibetan, shedding Chinese terms from their vocabulary. In Sertha, elders were handing out free dictionaries to youngsters. Writers and musicians in eastern Tibet, many of whom used to prefer the Chinese language as their artistic medium, now compose and perform predominantly in Tibetan. In certain restaurants and cafes, owners serve customers only when they order in Tibetan. Netizens on Weibo (the Chinese version of Twitter) and Renren (the Chinese version of Facebook) tweet in Tibetan, regularly posting politically charged images and poems online.[134] By the time Chinese censors detect and block them, these memes and messages have already reached their audience and served their purpose. For example, every July, memes celebrating the Dalai Lama's birthday would populate websites and social media platforms such as Youku (the Chinese version of YouTube) and Weibo for a few hours before being taken down.

Noncooperation

For decades, the predominant tactic in Tibetan resistance has been the street protest. Though an effective and low-risk tactic in exile, the cost of street protests within Tibet is staggering. In turn, the Lhakar Movement's emphasis on more strategic forms of resistance has enabled Tibetans to appreciate the power of noncooperation. Since

---

[133] Radio Free Asia, "Tibetan Private School Ordered Shut in China's Qinghai Province," 8 May 2014; and "Tibetan Language Promotion Event Blocked by China," 22 April 2014.
[134] *The Economist*, "Tibetan Blogging: Tweets from the Plateau," 18 August 2012.

2008, many Tibetans have started eating only in Tibetan restaurants and buying only from Tibetan shops, prompting Chinese businesses to close down in several towns including nationalist hotbeds like Dranggo and Ngaba (see Figure 3 in Chapter 3).[135] In early 2011, a group of Tibetans started boycotting the Chinese vegetable shops in Nangchen, where a monopoly of the market by Chinese vendors had enabled them to grossly overcharge. Within two months of the boycott, many of the Chinese groceries closed down for lack of business. In their place, new Tibetan vegetable vendors popped up.[136]

For the first time in recent memory, Tibetans are seeing how their individual actions as consumers can change their collective wellbeing and influence. The discourse of resistance is shifting from one of victimhood to one that emphasizes agency, creativity and strategy. Empowered by the tangible results of noncooperation, Tibetans have expanded their concept of nonviolent resistance beyond religiously driven commitment to nonviolence, to incorporate strategy and tactical innovation.

---

[135] This information is based on a recent interview that the author conducted with a highly informed Tibetan in exile.
[136] Radio Free Asia, "Tibetans Boycott Chinese Shops," 12 April 2011.

Chapter 8
A Comparison of the Three Uprisings

Referring to Sharp's typology of nonviolent methods (see Figure 1 in Chapter 1), this section compares three uprisings and highlights how they differed from one another with regard to the use of nonviolent tactics. By examining this, we can graph the evolution of the Tibetan commitment to nonviolent resistance over the course of half a century. The total number of different types of nonviolent tactics used by Tibetans increased from 22 in the first uprising, to 43 in the second, to 59 in the third. From this chart alone, one can conclude that the Tibetans' practice of nonviolent resistance and the embrace of nonviolent discipline has clearly grown more robust, proactive and strategic over the last 60 years.

Figure 4. Number of Nonviolent Tactics Used in the Three Tibetan Uprisings

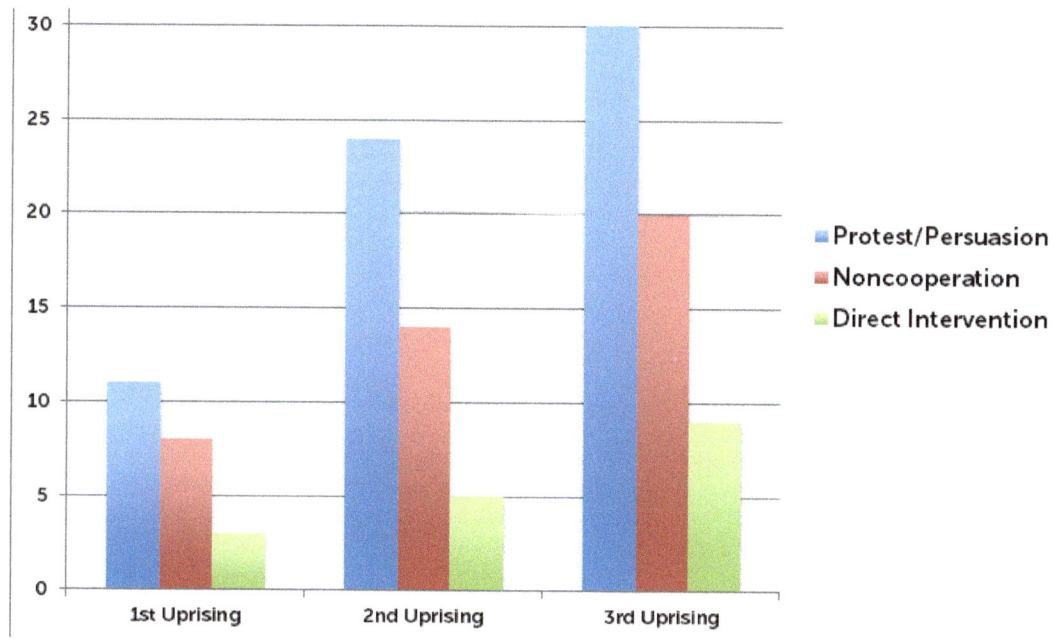

Source: Author

Figure 5. Nonviolent Tactics/Methods Used by Tibetans in the Uprisings

METHODS OF PROTEST AND PERSUASION	1956-59	1987-89	2008-13
Public speeches	✓	✓	✓
Letters of opposition or support	✓	✓	✓
Declarations by organizations and institutions	✓	✓	✓
Signed public statements	✓	✓	✓
Group or mass petitions	✓	✓	✓
Slogans, caricatures and symbols	✓	✓	✓
Banners, poster and displayed communications		✓	✓
Leaflets, pamphlets and books	✓	✓	✓
Newspapers and journals	✓	✓	✓
Records, radio and television		✓	✓
Skywriting and earth writing		✓	
Displays of flags and symbolic colors	✓	✓	✓
Wearing of symbols		✓	✓
Prayer and worship		✓	✓
Destruction of own property			✓
Displays of portraits			✓
Paint as protest			✓
Symbolic reclamations		✓	✓
Rude gestures		✓	✓
Vigils	✓	✓	✓
Singing		✓	✓
Marches	✓	✓	✓
Religious processions			✓
Motorcades			✓
Political mourning		✓	✓
Demonstrative funerals		✓	✓
Assemblies of protest or support		✓	✓
Protest meetings			✓
Teach-ins			✓
Walk-outs		✓	✓
Silence		✓	✓

Chapter 8: A Comparison of the Three Uprisings

METHODS OF NONCOOPERATION	1956-59	1987-89	2008-13
Social boycott	✓	✓	✓
Selective social boycott			✓
Interdict			✓
Boycott of social affairs			✓
Withdrawal from social institutions		✓	✓
Stay-at-home		✓	✓
Total personal noncooperation		✓	✓
Protest emigration	✓	✓	
Consumers' boycott			✓
Refusal to let or sell property	✓	✓	✓
Refusal of a government's money		✓	✓
Blacklisting of traders			✓
Peasant strike			✓
Prisoners' strike		✓	✓
Withholding or withdrawal of allegiance	✓	✓	✓
Literature and speeches advocating resistance		✓	✓
Withdrawal from government educational institutions		✓	✓
Refusal to dissolve existing institutions	✓	✓	✓
Refusal of an assemblage or meeting to disperse	✓	✓	✓
Sit-down	✓		✓
Hiding, escape and false identities	✓	✓	✓

METHODS OF NONVIOLENT INTERVENTION	1956-59	1987-89	2008-13
The fast		✓	✓
Nonviolent obstruction	✓	✓	✓
Nonviolent occupation	✓	✓	✓
Establishing new social patterns			✓
Alternative social institutions			✓
Alternative communication system		✓	✓
Alternative markets			✓
Seeking imprisonment			✓
Dual sovereignty and parallel government	✓	✓	✓

Figure 5 shows that in the first uprising, Tibetans only managed to use a handful of nonviolent resistance tactics. There are many reasons behind this, including a lack of political consciousness, a low degree of urbanization, poor communication exacerbated by hostile terrain, and a delay in technological progress. Moreover, during this uprising, Tibetans were using nonviolent tactics merely as supplementary tools to aid the armed resistance. In the second uprising, we can see a sharp rise in the different types of tactics used, from 22 to 43 types. By this time, the Tibetan exile leadership had cemented its commitment to nonviolence, and the monk activists in Tibet did their best to maintain nonviolent discipline – and they did so successfully except for the occasional lapse such as the property destruction committed by lay Tibetans who joined the demonstrations. In the third uprising, the language of nonviolent resistance became deeply embedded in the Tibetan national discourse. With the translation of Sharp's works in the late 1990s, a number of terms related to civil resistance entered the Tibetan lingo. For example, the term nonviolent conflict can be translated as ཞི་བའི་ཐབ་རྩོད (shi-wei thap-tsoe); civil resistance as སྤྱི་མང་གི་གོག་འོལ (chi-mang gi gog-ol); and strategic nonviolent action as འཐབ་བྱུས་ལྡན་པའི་ཞི་བའི་ལས་འགུལ (thap-ju denpey shi-wei ley-gul).

The Tibetans have employed not only more types of protest tactics, but also a greater number of noncooperation and intervention tactics. This can be explained in part by the fact that Tibetans are now more familiar with stories of nonviolent resistance in other countries, and the lessons that can be learned from the successes and mistakes of other struggles. The improved channels of trans-Himalayan communication, thanks to platforms such as the Tibetan radio services and the proliferation of digital tools, played a critical role in moving the Tibetan nonviolent resistance toward greater strategic and tactical sophistication.

While the first uprising was a direct response to China's attack on religion and thus a reactive uprising in which religion was the epicenter of mobilization, the second was a more proactive campaign where the central theme was political rather than religious (see Figure 6). The third uprising, and the period immediately preceding it and following it, revolved around culture as the epicenter of resistance, with demands including freedom and independence for Tibet and the return of the Dalai Lama. During this period, Tibetans also began to engage in more self-reflective and self-reliance campaigns that seek to strengthen the fabric of Tibetan society, culture and economy.

Chapter 8: A Comparison of the Three Uprisings

Figure 6. Characteristics of the Three Tibetan Uprisings

	1st Uprising: 1956-59	2nd Uprising: 1987-89	3rd Uprising: 2008-13
Dominant theme	Religious	Political	Cultural
Catalyst	His Holiness The Dalai Lama's (HHDL) life in danger	HHDL's reputation attacked by China	Beijing Olympics
Method	Armed struggle	Nonviolent (some incidents ended in riots)	Nonviolent (15 out of 200 involved property destruction)
Nonviolent tactics used	22	43	59
Geographic scope	Nationwide	Lhasa and Central Tibet	Nationwide
Slogan, demands	China out of Tibet, Independence for Tibet	Independence for Tibet, Long Live HHDL	Return of HHDL to Tibet, Independence, Freedom, Language Freedom, Equality
Tibetan casualties	87,000 dead in the 1959 uprising, thousands imprisoned in the aftermath	Thousands imprisoned, number of dead not fully known. *The Observer* reported that according to a report from the Public Security Bureau and the Tibet Military District Command dated March 11, 1989, "387 Lhasa citizens have been killed . . . 721 were injured, 2,100 have been arrested or detained . . . 354 have disappeared. . . 82 religious people have been killed, 37 injured, 650 arrested or detained."	The Tibetan Center for Human Rights and Democracy registered more than 135 Tibetans deaths as a direct result of armed retaliation by law enforcement forces. Thousands imprisoned in Central Tibet, Kham and Amdo. In Kanlho (Gannan) Prefecture alone, a total of 2,644 Tibetans were arrested between March 14 and April 9, 2008.

	1st Uprising: 1956-59	2nd Uprising: 1987-89	3rd Uprising: 2008-13
Chinese casualties	Precise number unknown, but can be estimated to run into the tens of thousands as a result of the Tibetan guerrilla war	0-5	Too many conflicting numbers
Tools of communication and mobilization	Word of mouth	Word of mouth, radio	Word of mouth, mobile phones, QQ (a Chinese version of Skype), radio
Level of internal organization, networking, and communication within the movement before and during the uprising	Medium	Low	Medium

Note: For methodology, see page 10

Chapter 9
Strategic Challenges and Transformative Resistance

In the past six decades, the Tibetan freedom struggle has gone through various phases: armed resistance, internationalization, nonviolent escalation, de-escalation, dialogue, and finally, grassroots cultural resistance. The Tibetan government has pursued a range of strategies: cooperation with the Chinese in the 1950s; the mobilization of Western support in the 1980s and 90s; appeasement and dialogue in the first decade of the 21st century; grassroots outreach to the Chinese public in the last few years;[137] and finally, increasing visibility of alternative, creative forms of nonviolent resistance via cultural and economic self-organization that are evolving independently of the formal Tibetan leadership — or, perhaps, in spite of it.

What emerges from this strategic and historical review of the struggle is that the Tibetan leadership and public have universally committed to nonviolent credo of their actions but suffered from conflicting strategies. Nevertheless, this process may be precisely what made the path to transformative resistance a feasible alternative.

Nonviolent Credo and Existing Strategic Challenges

Ever since the Tibetan government's renunciation of violent means in 1974 — marked by the closing of the Mustang guerrilla base — Tibetans have consistently pursued a nonviolent path in their struggle for freedom. Not only has the Tibetan government demonstrated a genuine commitment to nonviolent discipline in all its initiatives, but Tibetan advocacy groups and NGOs have also embraced nonviolent means as indispensable to the struggle. Tibetans have witnessed firsthand — especially

---

[137] At the urging of the Dalai Lama, some Tibetan communities in exile have set up Chinese-Tibetan Friendship Associations. But to date, the centerpiece of this strategy is the Dalai Lama himself, who holds numerous meetings, both private and public, with Chinese citizens, students and democrats.

during the 2008 uprising – that any lapse in nonviolent discipline gives the Chinese government the ammunition to delegitimize the Tibetan struggle and to justify Beijing's heavy-handed repression.

To date, there has not been a single cohesive Tibetan group since 1974 (when the Mustang guerrilla base was shut down) that has waged a violent campaign. In spite of China's routine accusations of terrorism levied against the Tibetan Youth Congress, the group has never used violence in its activities. The most controversial tactic in the Tibetan Youth Congress arsenal remains the hunger strike, which is not only nonviolent but a tactic closely associated with Gandhi, a world-renowned exemplar of nonviolent resistance. Thus the Tibetan government and the public have shown close alignment with each other in their faith in nonviolent discipline and actions.

In spite of the broad consensus around nonviolent discipline, one of the major weaknesses of the movement has been a consistent disconnect between the strategies employed by the Tibetan leadership and the Tibetan public. In the 1950s, when the Khampa guerrillas waged armed resistance against Chinese invasion, the government in Lhasa cooperated with the Chinese and did not support the "rebels." From 1987 to 1993, while Tibetan demonstrators in Lhasa overwhelming called for Tibetan independence, the Dalai Lama had already launched his Middle Way Proposal and conceded independence in favor of autonomy. At the turn of the millennium, when Tibetan advocacy groups and communities in the West adopted a strategy of shaming Chinese leaders during their overseas trips, the Tibetan government discouraged the protests, arguing that they would not be conducive to Sino-Tibetan dialogue. In the lead up to the 2008 Beijing Olympics, when the Tibetan public and grassroots activists organized high-profile protests in and outside China, the Tibetan leadership adopted a more neutral stance, emphasizing diplomacy and negotiations over civil resistance and disruption of the Olympic Games.

The Tibetan government's fundamental strategy revolves around trying to convert the Chinese leadership. Its actions are aimed at persuading the Chinese government through display of goodwill, compassion and trust building, to compromise on Tibet. Accordingly, Dharamsala's campaigns have relied heavily on the use of persuasive diplomacy to appeal to the Chinese leaders' humanity. In contrast, the grassroots movement's strategy is one of imposing costs, escalating pressure and forcing changes to oppressive policies and practices. The grassroots movement focuses on shifting the cost-benefit calculus of the Chinese leaders and their supporters over a continued harsh occupation of Tibet, and ultimately coercing change through organized nonviolent, disruptive and creative pressure.

Since 2008, the target of the Tibetan leadership's persuasive diplomacy shifted from the Chinese government to the Chinese public. In a speech in October 2008, the Dalai Lama said, "I have not lost faith in the people of China but my faith in the present Chinese government is thinning and it's becoming very difficult."[138] The Tibetan leadership began encouraging its public to engage in grassroots outreach to the Chinese public. But outreach to the Chinese has remained mostly an exile-oriented initiative and largely symbolic. It rarely goes beyond formal statements of solidarity, expressions of support and the mandatory photo-ops.

On the other hand, there are very few signs of Tibetans in Tibet organizing grassroots outreach to Chinese citizens to find common grievances around which to rally. The cultural, linguistic, occupational and social differences between Tibetans and Chinese continue to pose seemingly insurmountable obstacles for such endeavors to gain traction. Nevertheless, the potential benefits of strategic collaboration with certain sections of Chinese grassroots around issues of common concerns – for instance, the environmental devastation of Tibet, which causes flooding downstream, is as much a Chinese grievance as it is a Tibetan one – are too great to be written off yet.

Transformative Resistance

Perhaps because of the instinctive and subtle rejection of Dharamsala's diplomatic overtures to Beijing, the Tibetan grassroots today has increasingly turned toward what it thinks is more feasible, needed and effective to challenge the Chinese policies long term: Largely unknown to the world, it is engaged in a growing movement of transformative resistance. China's militarization and securitization of the Tibetan plateau, instead of extinguishing the Tibetan resistance, has sent it underground, firmly embedding it in the daily lives of ordinary individuals. The Lhakar movement has given birth to the transformative resistance, a form of resistance that some define as "a proactive effort to transform colonizer/colonized subjectivity, colonial discourses, and material structures."[139]

---

[138] Nicholas Kristof, "The Dalai Lama's Clarification," *The New York Times*, 28 October 2008.
[139] Abujidi Nurhan, *Urbicide in Palestine: Spaces of Oppression and Resilience* (New York: Routledge, 2014), 225.

From a movement that was largely built around expression of opposition to Chinese rule, the Tibetans have transformed their resistance into a more sophisticated struggle in which the focus is on mind, speech and action. Tibetan liberation from the colonized mindset is key to their political liberation. Instead of highlighting their resentment against Chinese presence in Tibet, Tibetans are channeling their antagonism into positive practices of self-improvement and self-empowerment, and use new narratives of Tibetan courage and creativity to shape a new discourse of hope and freedom. Initiatives include: launching Tibetan cooperatives; holding underground language classes; publishing underground literary magazines (Tibetan samizdat); turning to the local monastery instead of the local court to settle internal disputes; engaging in and popularizing Tibetan cultural and religious practices; and occupying the Jokhang Square on important religious occasions. These are only the most visible of a wide array of transformative programs that ordinary Tibetans are engaging in today. The fact that Tibetans are waging a quiet but resilient nonviolent movement in an immensely repressive political climate shows that there are ways to mobilize people power against even one of the most ruthless and powerful regimes in the world.

> *Tibetans have transformed their resistance into a more sophisticated struggle in which the focus is on mind, speech and action. Tibetan liberation from the colonized mindset is key to their political liberation.*

This type of everyday resistance, aimed at self-development, self-betterment and self-empowerment, does not rely on a particular institution for formal leadership. The decentralized and grassroots nature of such resistance allows the Tibetan public to exercise more autonomous, self-propelled leadership at the local level for the time being. Local leaders and regional organizers play an important role during this phase of transformative resistance, the outcomes of which can eventually translate into direct actions at the national level. As these local grassroots efforts increase the leverage of the nationwide movement, there is a growing importance of recognized pan-Tibetan leaders and their role in national-level campaigns that might pave the way for negotiations with the Chinese government from a position of strength.

Chapter 10
Recommendations for Domestic and External Actors

In spite of its shortcomings, the Tibetan leadership's strategy of internationalizing the cause in the 1980s rescued the Tibet issue from obscurity and propelled it into the limelight. However, when the Cold War ended and China emerged as an economic heavyweight, this strategy, which was premised on the capitalist West as the anti-communist defender of human rights, ran into obstacles. Western governments that condemned Beijing's massacre of its own students in Tiananmen Square in 1989, such as the US government, soon found themselves rushing to Beijing in the 1990s in their eagerness to sign lucrative trade deals with China. Moreover, while the Tibetan leadership overwhelmingly emphasized persuasive diplomacy, it underestimated the importance of mobilization and escalation that would enhance leverage over Beijing. Dharamsala needs to carry out a strategic soul-searching and draft a new long-term plan that plays to Tibetan strengths and exploits the Chinese regime's weaknesses.

The Tibetan government in exile, now being led by a lay prime minister[140] since the Dalai Lama's devolution of political authority, has the opportunity to replace Dharamsala's appeasement politics with a more forceful approach. Without the Dalai Lama's charisma, the new administration will find its mobilizing ability and sphere of influence circumscribed not only in foreign capitals but also inside Tibet. Nevertheless, Dharamsala's loss of charisma can be offset by investing in strategic planning, alliance building, the logistics of organizing, and most importantly, revitalizing the global grassroots movement for Tibet.

The Tibetan leadership must free itself from the religious worldview that had

---

[140] In 2012, Dr. Lobsang Sangay became the first lay prime minister of the Tibetan government in exile. He was democratically elected to this post by the Tibetan exile population, and his election was closely followed by Tibetans in Tibet as well.

shaped the vision of the struggle but also constrained actions in the past, and chart a new path firmly rooted in the tenets and practice of strategic nonviolent struggle. It must also replace its religious conceptualization of nonviolence with a more secular one, so that the emphasis is not merely on avoiding violence but on exploring and deploying, in a strategically shrewd sequence, a full spectrum of nonviolent methods. Such an approach would aim to mobilize a greater number of people both inside and outside of Tibet.

To force Beijing into genuine negotiations where the Chinese recognize the Tibetan side as an equal partner, Dharamsala must escalate the conflict through both continued strengthening of the Tibetan societal fabric and a growing nonviolent mobilization, including the use of creative and disruptive actions. It must let Beijing see that the costs of delaying a resolution can be prohibitively high for China. Dialogue/negotiation and escalation should not be seen as being mutually exclusive. In fact, the only way to bring Beijing into substantive dialogue is through escalation. The ultimate reason behind the current deadlock, after all, is not a lack of trust from Beijing's side, but a lack of heat under its feet.

A centrally coordinated, locally and internationally executed grassroots movement could reduce the human cost of activism in Tibet, encouraging low-risk actions over high-risk ones while emphasizing the strategic over the spontaneous. By promoting tactics of dispersion (such as strikes, boycotts, economic and social noncooperation) over those of concentration (protest marches, public gatherings), Dharamsala can not only reduce the cost but also increase the scope and sustainability of the movement. There are hundreds of low-risk, high-impact nonviolent tactics that Dharamsala could advocate, help Tibetans plan for and execute.

Additionally, a grassroots-oriented blueprint for escalation that assigns an important role to the Tibetan public inside Tibet may be an effective instrument to nudge some Tibetans away from acts of desperation and engage them in more intentional, coordinated, creative and life-affirming methods of challenging Chinese rule. The absence of a strategic plan often feeds feelings of disempowerment and leaves the movement to the mercy of its own spontaneous, uncoordinated outbursts of frustration and despair — feelings which may underlie some people's decision to engage in tragic tactics like self-immolation.

To increase its chances of success, the Tibetan leadership must recalibrate its strategy to harness not only international but also domestic societal forces. Eventually,

Chapter 10: Recommendations for Domestic and External Actors

the long-term objective of a self-managed Tibetan society in Tibet would be to challenge the centralized power of the Chinese state without necessarily confronting it directly. Grassroots cultural, economic and social activism could gradually, if not stealthily, shift the authority away from the Chinese regime to Tibetans themselves. Tibetans could thus make Tibet governable for themselves. At the same time, a self-organized Tibetan society could hollow out the power of Chinese governability over the region and its people. Tibetans could reclaim their power through mobilization of their internal forces, and with this newly acquired strength multiply the pressure on China. Considering the disproportionate power between parties, this could prove a more effective way to leverage Tibetans' influence and force the highly intransigent Chinese regime to enter into negotiations in good faith.

> *The Tibetan leadership would do well to embrace its role as a leader and organizer of the movement rather than just a spokesperson for the issue.*

Although many Tibetans may feel that the Tibetan resistance movement has exhausted the tools of nonviolent resistance, this study makes it clear that the movement has explored only part of the great inventory of nonviolent weaponry. What the struggle needs most at the present moment is a stronger alignment of strategy between the Tibetan leadership and the grassroots. The Tibetan leadership would do well to embrace its role as a leader and organizer of the movement rather than just a spokesperson for the issue. It could treat the Tibetan grassroots as a nonviolent army of dedicated activists whose resistance it could guide and coordinate, rather than as a mass of suffering victims whose actions it must restrain. Tibetans themselves are yet to explore the numerous nonviolent methods such as social boycott and economic noncooperation, which are low-cost but high-impact. The Tibetan leadership has never planned for or explicitly encouraged such actions.

What Foreign Actors Can Do

Increase refugee assistance: The role that foreign countries, governments and institutions can play in supporting the Tibetan struggle cannot be underestimated. It goes without saying that the financial assistance from India, the United States and European countries has helped the Tibetan refugee community to survive and the exile institutions to exist for the past six decades. These programs of humanitarian assistance must be continued, and if possible, expanded. However, to truly help the sick, one must not only treat the symptoms but also cure the disease. Foreign actors' support for Tibet, therefore, must go beyond projects that are merely humanitarian in nature and actively promote and endorse the actions specified below.

Recognize the Tibetan government in exile: Although the Dalai Lama devolved his political authority in 2012, he continues to be universally recognized as the leader and spokesperson of the Tibetan people. The Tibetan government in exile, on the contrary, does not enjoy the same recognition on the global stage. The legitimacy earned by the Dalai Lama has been of immense service to the Tibetan cause, but it will endure only as long as he lives. Institutional legitimacy, on the other hand, can endure beyond the lifespan of an individual. Therefore, foreign governments should extend greater recognition toward the Tibetan government, the Tibetan parliament in exile, and develop stronger relationships with Tibetan exile institutions. Foreign heads of state should schedule an official meeting with the Tibetan Prime Minister each time they visit India and/or extend official invitations to the Tibetan prime minister to visit them in their respective capitals. If they are overly concerned about the Chinese government's reaction, in the beginning, they might choose unconventional settings such as the 'drop-in' meetings that President Clinton was fond of using.[141] Foreign members of Parliaments and US Congress should meet and greet Tibetan members of Parliament from Dharamsala in public settings, not only to send a message to China, but more importantly to build a long-term relationship with the institution of the Tibetan government as the legitimate representative of the Tibetan people both in and outside Tibet.

Recognize Tibetan movement leaders: Foreign actors can support the Tibetan freedom struggle by recognizing those making the greatest sacrifices. Rights organizations and foundations, and even government bodies, should recognize Tibetan political prisoners, writers, musicians and leaders through awards, tributes and honors.

---

[141] President Clinton used this 'drop-in' tactic several times to make his meetings with the Dalai Lama more acceptable to Chinese leaders. This is how it worked: Vice President Al Gore would arrange to meet the Dalai Lama in his office, and then a few minutes into the meeting, President Clinton would casually drop in. This supposedly allowed him to meet with the Dalai Lama without ruffling Beijing's feathers.

Chapter 10: Recommendations for Domestic and External Actors

In 2013, the US State Department set an example in this regard by presenting the 'International Women of Courage' award to Woeser, the Beijing-based Tibetan writer and activist. In 2014, the Oslo Freedom Forum awarded Dhondup Wangchen, Tibetan political prisoner, with the Václav Havel International Prize for Creative Dissent. These symbolic gestures raise the profile of Tibetan activists and resistance leaders in Tibet, giving them a layer of protection from Beijing's wrath, and sometimes better treatment in prison. These highly visible international solidarity actions help give Tibetans in the frontlines of activism more breathing room and a better chance of physical as well as mental survival, so that they may continue their struggle.

Shift the discourse about the Tibetan struggle to that of self-determination and decolonization: While discourse is not the same as concrete, on-the-ground action, the former informs and propels the latter. Consequently, foreign governments, parliaments and institutions should reframe the Tibet issue in the language of self-determination and decolonization. The current discourse casts Tibet as a problem of human rights, cultural preservation or religious freedom, thereby drastically reducing the scope of discussion as well as action on the subject. Reframing Tibet as a problem of self-determination or decolonization will make possible a more expansive discussion of the subject in any forum, put China on the defensive, and allow the free world to engage with China from a position of strength. National parliaments should, whenever possible, pass legislation that reaffirms Tibet's history as an independent country. For one, Tibet's independent past is a matter of principle for many Tibetans, particularly younger generation. More pertinently, insisting on Tibet's historical sovereignty sets a strong starting point for any possible negotiations with the Chinese regime, and carves out as much space as possible to discuss other issues.

Introduce sanctions: Parliaments can pass legislation calling for targeted sanctions against specific Chinese political and military leaders who are directly responsible for egregious crimes against Tibetans. Although the top Chinese leaders may be legally protected from these punitive measures, mid-level decision-makers and implementers can be subject to sanction measures such as visa bans and asset freeze. The US-led sanctions against the Burmese military junta included similar punitive measures that denied Burmese generals perks such as being able to travel to the West or invest in the global stock market. Naturally, China is not Burma, and sanctions against the Chinese

top-brass seem unlikely, but this should not prevent governments from developing and publishing a black list of Chinese local and regional officials (both military and political) who are directly responsible for human rights violations of Tibetans in Tibet. Nuanced sanctions targeting mid-level Chinese officials are far from impossible. In fact, in 2014, US Congressmen Jim McGovern and Joseph Pitts introduced the Reciprocal Access to Tibet Act, a bill that "would deny access to the United States by Chinese officials who are responsible for creating or administering restrictive policies on travel to Tibetan areas until China eliminates discriminatory restrictions on access by Americans to Tibet."[142]

Ignore China's hypersensitivity: Foreign governments and institutions should be aware of China's strategic use of hypersensitivity as a weapon of foreign policy. Over the last two decades, the Chinese leadership has unfailingly expressed its hurt as well as outrage at the slightest sign of foreign support for Tibet, even when the nature of the support is purely humanitarian. China often claims that statements supporting Tibetan human rights "hurt the feelings of the Chinese people."[143] Unfortunately, many politicians in the free world have naively accepted the supposedly Chinese notion of 'saving face,' and have gone out of their way to insulate Chinese leaders from any situation that might be mildly embarrassing for them during their foreign travels. In reality, Chinese leaders have intentionally cultivated this strategic hypersensitivity and are using it as a weapon to silence criticism and promote self-censorship on the part of democratic countries. Therefore, foreign actors that seek to support Tibet must learn to ignore China's temper tantrums as empty threats and not allow Beijing to use this false hypersensitivity as an instrument that attempts to remove the Tibet issue from the domestic and global public consciousness.

What the Tibetan Leadership Can Do

Control the discourse: The Tibetan leadership's greatest success has been its

---

[142] International Campaign for Tibet, "ICT welcomes U.S. legislation to promote access to Tibet," 12 June 2014, http://www.savetibet.org/ict-welcomes-u-s-legislation-to-promote-access-to-tibet/.

[143] In 2007, the author was part of a team of Tibetan activists who staged a protest at a Mt. Everest base camp against China's occupation of Tibet. After detaining the group for three days, the Chinese police made them sign a statement saying that they were sorry to "hurt the feelings of the Chinese people."

Chapter 10: Recommendations for Domestic and External Actors

ability to shape the discourse on Tibet for almost half a century in the global media, academic forums and the public arena.[144] However, over the last decade, the Chinese government has waged an aggressive public relations campaign to take control of Tibet-related discourse in the international and domestic halls of political power and in academic and media circles. As a result of China's investment in this campaign, the space for all discourse on Tibet has shrunk significantly in the various political arenas, academic institutions and news organizations. And whatever limited discussions do take place within narrow parameters dictated by Beijing are often pro-China.[145]

The Tibetan leadership must draft a long-term plan to reclaim the discourse on Tibet, invest in Tibetan and pro-Tibet scholars pursuing higher studies in various universities, and incentivize young Tibetans with residency and citizenship in other countries to run for positions in local and national legislative and executive bodies and choose professions like journalism. Many of the best Tibetan minds of our generation who have moved to the West have opted for "safer" professions, particularly in medicine. While caring for the sick is one of the noblest professions, it is important for the Tibetan leadership to proactively encourage the younger generation of Tibetans to seek careers in diverse and underrepresented professional fields such as business, politics, journalism, education, law, etc. Politicians, lobbyists, writers, academics and artists are well-positioned to influence the discourse and public opinion on Tibet, and thus propel action and effect change on the issue.

Activate the allies: There is no doubt that Tibetans have many allies and potential allies. The question is: how can the Tibetan leadership activate its allies and harness their abilities? Each of these communities of supporters – friends in foreign parliaments, the business community, the art and entertainmentindustry, and the global Buddhist

---

[144] At a 2000 Chinese government conference on external propaganda and Tibetology work, the Minister of Information Office of China's State Council, Zhao Qizheng said, "During every foreign visit of our leaders last year, the Dalai clique, with covert incitement and help from Western countries as well as Tibet Support Groups, interfered and created disruption through protest rallies. In this way, they gained the highest-level international platform and intervention." See footnote 111 in Chapter 7 for more details and a link to the leaked statement.

[145] In many elite universities, the discourse on Tibet has turned pro-China in recent years, as more Confucius Institutes have propped up on campuses. Universities are more hesitant than ever to invite the Dalai Lama to speak on their campuses. In 2013, Sydney University even attempted to cancel a Dalai Lama event after pressure from China. At global educational institutions like the Asia Society, discussions related to Tibet are conducted in an intentionally depoliticized manner and language.

community – has something different to contribute to the Tibetan struggle. When the Zenko-ji temple in Japan took a stand on Tibet in 2008 and refused to host the Chinese Olympic torch, causing much embarrassment to Beijing, it offered a small glimpse into the Buddhist community's potential to support Tibet, if only Tibetans are willing to tap into it.[146] The Tibetan leadership must not let the Buddhist notion of modesty and contentment limit the kinds of support it can ask from its friends and allies. No one ever got more by asking for less. Tibetans should ask parliamentarians for bolder statements, governments for stronger actions, and rights groups to do more for Tibet. One of the greatest strengths of the Tibetan struggle is the grassroots Tibet Support Groups that emerged in the 1980s and 90s, many of whom have disappeared amid economic woes and negligence from Dharamsala. The Tibetan leadership should reactivate this important community, whose skills, diligence and networks form an essential part of the Tibetan struggle.

> *The Tibetan leadership must not let the Buddhist notion of modesty and contentment limit the kinds of support it can ask from its friends and allies.*

Mobilize the masses: The Tibetan leadership must play a more active role immobilizing the Tibetan public both in Tibet and in exile to take part in strategically devised campaigns aimed at strengthening the Tibetan society in Tibet while weakening Beijing's formal authority in the region. Dharamsala could help plan for deployment of hundreds of low-risk, high-impact nonviolent tactics to make Tibet less governable for China and more controllable for Tibetans, thus raising China's political and financial cost of oppressing Tibet. Dharamsala's moral reservations about mobilizing Tibetans in Tibet, due to the human cost that goes with it, are understandable and admirable. But the bitter truth is that a grassroots-oriented plan for escalation that engages the Tibetan public in Tibet is perhaps the only way to nudge Tibetans away from acts of desperation and towards hopeful and life-affirming ways of challenging Chinese rule. The notion that mobilization of grassroots and escalation of conflict will hurt Sino-Tibetan dialogue

---

[146] Chisaki Watanabe, "Japanese Buddhist temple refuses Olympic torch," *USA Today*, 18 April 2008, http://usatoday30.usatoday.com/news/world/2008-04-18-1127293845_x.htm.

Chapter 10: Recommendations for Domestic and External Actors

should by now be understood as pure, and tragically misleading, myth. In reality, greater mobilization of the masses, greater self-organization of Tibetan society and escalation of nonviolent pressure are the only real leverages that the Tibetan government has to push Beijing toward more genuine negotiations.

Explore legal avenues: It is for good reason that we often lament the weakness of international law, a shortcoming that is epitomized by the United Nations' failure to address the Tibet issue. However, there are other legal tools and systems that could be used more creatively by the Tibetan leadership. The best example in this regard was set by a Tibetan monk in Spain who, with the help of Spanish lawyers acting for the Spanish NGO Comite de Apoyo al Tibet, filed a lawsuit against former Chinese leaders for crimes against humanity.[147] In 2013, in a move that shocked many legal experts, the Spanish National Court ordered arrest warrants to be issued against five former Chinese leaders including Jiang Zemin.[148] Although Spain later dropped the judicial investigation due to political pressure, what the BBC described as the Tibetan "genocide" lawsuit against top Chinese leaders was a major humiliation for China.[149] The practical domain of universal jurisdiction, while small, is expanding, and several countries in the European Union and Latin America already apply the principle in practice. Instead of discouraging such lawsuits for fear of offending Beijing, the Tibetan leadership must encourage its support groups around the world to pursue legal avenues of seeking justice for the Tibetan people.

The above recommendations are by no means an exhaustive list of what the Tibetan leadership and external actors can do to help the Tibetan struggle. It is a modest list of recommended actions that Dharamsala and its foreign allies could pursue to come up with more effective policies and programs that raise pressure on Beijing to compromise and advance the struggle for a free Tibet.

---

[147] The Tibetan monk Thupten Wangchen was helped by Tibet activist Alan Cantos and legal expert Jose Esteve in launching this historic lawsuit that sought to apply the concept of universal jurisdiction to hold Chinese leaders accountable for their crimes in Tibet.

[148] International Campaign for Tibet, "Spanish criminal court orders arrest warrants against Chinese leaders following Hu Jintao indictment for Tibet policies," 18 November 2013. Read more at: http://www.savetibet.org/spanish-criminal-court-orders-arrest-warrants-against-chinese-leaders-following-hu-jintao-indictment-for-tibet-policies/.

[149] BBC News, "Spain drops 'genocide' case against China's Tibet leaders," 24 June 2014, http://www.bbc.com/news/world-asia-china-28000937.

Cited Literature

Abujidi, Nurhan, *Urbicide in Palestine: Spaces of Oppression and Resilience* (New York: Routledge, 2014).

Barnett, Robert, "Violated Specialness: Western Political Representations on Tibet" in *Imagining Tibet: Perceptions, Projections and Fantasies*, ed. Dodin and Rather (Boston: Wisdom Publications, 2001).

Bartkowski, Maciej J., "Recovering Nonviolent History," in *Recovering Nonviolent History: Civil Resistance in Liberation Struggles* ed. Maciej J. Bartkowski (Boulder: Lynne Rienner Publishers, 2013).

Beckwith, Christopher, "The Tibetans in the Ordos and North China: Considerations on the Role of the Tibetan Empire," in *World History*. http://himalaya.socanth.cam.ac.uk/collections/journals/jts/pdf/JTS_SL_01.pdf

Chao, Shan, "Sunshine after Rain," in *Peking Review*, 5 May 1950.

Chen, Jian, "The Tibetan Rebellion of 1959 and China's Changing Relations with India and the Soviet Union," in the *Journal of Cold War Studies*, Volume 8 Issue 3 Summer 2006, Cold War Studies at Harvard University.

Chenoweth, Erica and Maria J. Stephan, *Why Civil Resistance Works: The Strategic Logic of Nonviolent Conflict* (New York: Columbia University Press, 2011).

China Tibetology Research Center via *People's Daily*, "Report on the Economic and Social Development of Tibet," 30 March 2009, http://en.people.cn/90001/90776/90785/6625577.html.

Congressional-Executive Commission on China, Qinghai-Tibet Railway Statistics Add to Confusion, Mask Impact on Local Population, March 4, 2010.

Demick, Barbara, "In Tibet, A Worm Worth Its Weight in Gold," *Los Angeles Times*, 27 June 2008, http://www.latimes.com/world/asia/la-fg-worm27-2008jun27-story.html#page=1.

Department of Information and International Relations, International Resolutions and Recognitions on Tibet: 1959-1997.

Dorjee, Tenzin, "Why Lhakar Matters: The Elements of Tibetan Freedom," in *Tibetan Political Review*, 10 January 2013, http://www.tibetanpoliticalreview.org/articles/whylhakarmatterstheelementsoftibetanfreedom.

Fischer, David Hackett, *Paul Revere's Ride* (Oxford University Press, 1995).

Goldstein, Melvyn, *The Snow Lion and the Dragon: China, Tibet and the Dalai Lama*, (Berkeley: University of California Press, 1997).

Grunfeld, Tom, *The Making of Modern Tibet* (New York: M.E. Sharpe, 1996).

Huerta-Sanchez, Emilia et al. "Altitude adaptation in Tibetans caused by introgression of Denisovan-like DNA," in *Nature* 512, (14 August 2014).

International Court of Justice Report on Tibet, 1960.

Karmay, Samten, The Great Fifth, IIAS Newsletter #39.

Knaus, Kenneth, *Orphans of the Cold War* (Public Affairs, 1999).

Los Angeles Times Blog, Tibet activist Erin Potts' pays tribute to Adam Yauch, 8 May 2012.

Mallaby, Sebastian, "NGOs: Fighting Poverty, Hurting the Poor," *Foreign Policy Magazine*, September/October 2004.

McGranahan, Carole, *Arrested Histories: Tibet, the CIA, and Memories of a Forgotten War* (Duke University Press, 2010).

Moraes, Frank, *Revolt in Tibet* (New York: The Macmillan Company, 1960).

Morcom, Anna, *Unity and Discord: Music and Politics in Contemporary Tibet* (Tibet Information Network).

Motlagh, Jason, "Young Tibetans question path of nonviolence," in *The Christian Science Monitor*, 1 April 2008, http://www.csmonitor.com/World/Asia-Pacific/2008/0401/p01s01-woap.html.

Nonviolence International, *Truth is Our Only Weapon: The Tibetan Nonviolent Struggle*, (Bangkok, August 2000).

Norbu, Jamyang, *Shadow Tibet: Selected Writings 1989-2004* (High Asia Press, 2007).

Pandey, Geeta, "Exiles question Dalai Lama's non-violence," in *BBC News*, 18 March 2008, http://news.bbc.co.uk/2/hi/south_asia/7302661.stm.

Pempa, Dechen, "Waterfall of Youth – Dhondup Gyal," *High Peaks Pure Earth*, 16 February 2011, http://highpeakspureearth.com/2011/waterfall-of-youth-dhondup-gyal-music-video-by-yudrug-green-dragon/.

Pittsburgh Post-Gazette, "World Bank rejects controversial loan to China," 8 July 2000.

Popovic, Merriman, and Marovic, et al., *Canvas Core Curriculum: A Guide to Effective Nonviolent Struggle* (Belgrade: Center for Applied Nonviolent Action and Strategies, 2007).

Probe International Journal, "World Bank cancels China Tibet resettlement scheme," November 1999.

Radio Free Asia, "Tibetan Private School Ordered Shut in China's Qinghai Province," 8

May 2014.

Radio Free Asia, "Tibetans Boycott Chinese Shops," 12 April 2011.

Rossabi, Morris, *China Among Equals* (University of California Press, 1983).

Schaik, Sam van, *Tibet: A History* (Yale University Press, 2011).

Schwartz, Ronald, *Circle of Protest* (New York: Columbia University Press, 1994).

Shakabpa, W.D., *Tibet: A Political History* (New York: Potala Publications, 1984).

Shakya, Tsering, *The Dragon in the Land of Snows: A History of Modern Tibet Since 1947*, (New York: Columbia University Press, 1999).

Smith, Warren, *China's Tibet? Autonomy or Assimilation* (Rowman & Littlefield Publishers, 2008).

Sperling, Elliott, *The China-Tibet Conflict: History and Polemics*, East-West Center.

Sperling, Elliott, "Orientalism and Aspects of Violence in the Tibetan Tradition," in *Imagining Tibet: Perceptions, Projections and Fantasies*, ed. Dodin and Rather (Wisdom Publications, 2001).

Students for a Free Tibet, Leaked transcript of a speech delivered in 2000 by Zhao Qizheng, Minister of Information Office of China's State Council: https://studentsforafreetibet.org/get-involved/action-toolbox/tibet-related-external-propaganda-and-tibetology-work-in-the-new-era.

The Dalai Lama, *My Land and My People* (New York: Potala Publications, 1962).

The Dalai Lama's official website: http://www.dalailama.com/biography/travels.

The Economist, "Tibetan Blogging: Tweets from the Plateau," 18 August 2012.

The Tibetan and Himalayan Library, "A New Chapter in Tibetan Computing," http://www.thlib.org/tools/scripts/wiki/a%20new%20chapter%20in%20tibetan%20computing.html.

Tibet Information Network, *A Struggle of Blood and Fire: The Imposition of Martial Law in 1989 and the Lhasa Uprising in 1959* (1999).

Tibet Information Network, Reported Demonstrations 1987-96.

Tibet Justice Center, Legal Materials on Tibet.

Tibetan Center for Human Rights and Democracy, "Tibet Protests in 2008-2009: Profiles of Known Tibetans Who Died in the Protests," http://www.tchrd.org/wp-content/uploads/2013/03/tibet_protest_2010.pdf.

Timmons, Heather, "Tibetan Protest Marchers Vow to Reach Homeland," *The New York Times*, 12 March 2008.

Tsering, Tashi, "The Tibeto-Mongol Treaty of January 1913" in *Lungta Journal* Issue 17,

The Centennial of the Tibeto-Mongol Treaty: 1913-2013, Spring 2013.

Warner, Cameron, "Hope and Sorrow: Uncivil Religion, Tibetan Music Videos and YouTube," in *Ethnos: Journal of Anthropology*, 11 January 2013.

Yardley, Jim, "Violence in Tibet as monks clash with the police," *The New York Times*, 15 March 2008, http://www.nytimes.com/2008/03/15/world/asia/15tibet.html.

List of Figures

Figure 1. Methods of Nonviolent Action 14
Figure 2. Map of Tibetan Empire, circa 800 AD 20
Figure 3. Map of Tibetan Plateau with International and Disputed Boundaries 32
Figure 4. Number of Nonviolent Tactics Used in the Three Tibetan Uprisings 71
Figure 5. Nonviolent Tactics/Methods Used by Tibetans in the Three Uprisings 72
Figure 6. Characteristics of the Three Tibetan Uprisings 75

www.ingramcontent.com/pod-product-compliance
Lightning Source LLC
Chambersburg PA
CBHW041646040426
R18086900002B/R180869PG42333CBX00015B/5